Wanda, I [le] this book. I pray it will bless you!
Pastor Linda
Oct 7/2024

MW01135261

Unlocking

The Scriptures

Of Life

Gwen Titsworth

First Printing

Unlocking The Scriptures of Life

ISBN 978-0-9827825-0-7

Copyright © 2001, formerly *Life In The Scriptures: A Teaching Workbook* renamed 2010 by Gwen Titsworth

P.O. Box 1697
McAlester, Oklahoma 74502

Published by
Goldfinch Oracles, LLC
113 N. 1st Street
McAlester, Oklahoma 74501

Printed in the United States of America

All rights reserved under International Copyright Law. Contents and/or cover may not be reproduced in whole or in part in any form without the express written consent of the Publisher.

Contents

Dedication   i

Preface   ii

Chapter 1: Who or *What* is God/Man?   9

Chapter 2: Types and Shadows   15

Chapter 3: Genesis 1 - Seven Days of Creation   27

Chapter 4: The Coming of The Lord   55

Chapter 5: Born Again Man   71

Chapter 6: Why Did Jesus Die?   83

Chapter 7: Restored Life Eternal   95

Chapter 8: Kingdom of God   105

Chapter 9: The Bride   115

Chapter 10: Clouds of Glory   125

Chapter 11: Uncovering the Mystery   135

Chapter 12: End of The World   143

Chapter 13: Heaven or Hell?   151

    Darkness   152

    Fire   156

    Grave   162

    Hell   168

    Revelations 19-20   175

Benediction   193

Special Thanks   194

Dedication

With love and appreciation, I want to dedicate this book to the three greatest influences in my life.

Many thanks to my grandmother, Lillis Mize, who saw to it that I received the Word at an early age; to my natural mother, Gladys Wilkett, who introduced me to the Word of Life; to my spiritual mother, Alyce McPherson, who was my tutor and governor in the Word.

Preface

As far back as I can remember, I have had a love for God. At a young age, I would question why. Why did we have to die? What was the purpose for mankind to be born just to grow up to die? I was like Job; I just as soon 'not have been.' I knew there had to be more to God than what tradition had taught me. Years later, I found that there was a greater purpose for man's life through Christ.

As a teacher of The Word of Life, I have been asked several times by friends and family to write studies for them. With God's inspiration and guidance, I have compiled some of my teachings by putting in writing the depth of His Word as the Holy Spirit has revealed it to me and to others in this great day of the Lord. This will not be a book of great eloquence, but a spiritual study guide in the Word.

Each time before you begin to read this book, pray that the Spirit will open up the Word to you. Be sure to answer all the questions after each chapter. This will aid in planting the Word deep within your spirit and will cause you to begin to 'ponder the Word.'

My prayer is that the *Holy Spirit* will open your spiritual eyes to 'see' and will give you spiritual ears to 'hear' what the *Spirit* is saying. Traveling on the road of *Life* in truth will be one of the greatest journeys you will ever take. God bless you.

John 5: 39

Search the scriptures; for in them YE THINK ye have eternal life: and they are they which testify of me.

† *Chapter 1* †

Who or What is God/Man?

John 4:24 God is a Spirit: and they that worship him must worship him in spirit and in truth.

Before we can begin to understand God's Word or His language, we need to know who or what He is. From the above scripture, we see that God is a **Spirit**. Since you cannot compare apples to oranges, you cannot 'compare' God's spirit to man's carnality. *Romans 8:7* says the carnal mind is enmity or hostile against God. Either God will have to change or we will; and, I can assure you, it will not be God.

We have misunderstood for generations what God has been revealing to us in His Word concerning His plan and purpose for man. Why have we misunderstood? Because, we have tried to bring God to our level instead of going to His level or communicating with Him spirit to spirit. We must be in spirit to be in truth. I will cover this more extensively in another chapter.

1 Tim. 1:17 Now unto the King eternal, immortal, invisible, the only wise God, be honour and glory for ever and ever. Amen.

We see from the previous scripture that God is **eternal, immortal and invisible**. According to *Strong's*:

- *Eternal* means: an age, perpetuity, a Messianic period.

- *Immortal* means: un-decaying, not corruptible.

- *Invisible* means: incapable of being seen.

- *God* means: a deity, the supreme Divinity; figurative a magistrate.

There is **NOW** an unseen, incorruptible, perpetual Messianic age to be experienced and to appear through the magistrate. Other gods were worshipped by the people, but the true **God** was the only wise, eternal, immortal and invisible deity or magistrate. We cannot see God; but, we can see the effects of Him.

We now know that God is an **eternal, immortal, invisible** spirit. What is man? Job and David both asked this question.

Eccles. 12:7 Then shall the dust return to the earth as it was: and the spirit shall return unto God who gave it.

Our body is made of water, minerals and 'dirt.' The true 'us' is not 'body.' Our body is only a garment of skins to cover our spirit, as you would wear a coat for protection against the elements. We are spirit clothed with a body. What we truly are came from God, therefore, it will return to God. In the above scripture, it did not say any particular spirit would return to God, just the spirit.

1 Cor. 15:44 It is sown a natural body; it is raised a spiritual body. There is a natural body, and there is a spiritual body.

Psalm 139:13 For thou hast possessed my reins; thou hast covered me in my mother's womb.

- *Possessed* means: to erect, i.e. create.

- *Reins* means: a kidney; figurative the mind (as the interior self).

- *Covered* means: to entwine as a screen; to fence in, cover over, protect.

Our spirit, created and possessed by Him, is covered over in the womb. Spiritually, when we go through water baptism, we are sowing or burying the carnal man and being raised a new spiritual creation.

Heb. 12:6-9 For whom the Lord loveth he chasteneth, and scourgeth every son whom he receiveth.

- *Chasteneth* means: to train up, educate, discipline.

- *Scourgeth* means: to flog.

God disciplines, educates and trains up his children.

v. 7 If ye endure chastening, God dealeth with you as with sons; for what son is he whom the father chasteneth not?

- *Endure* means: to stay under, i.e. remain; figurative to undergo, i.e. bear (trials), have fortitude, persevere.

A true father will chasten his son. If you will remain in and have the fortitude to persevere the trials or chastening, you will become a mature son with the authority of the Father.

3

v. 8 But if ye be without chastisement, whereof all are partakers, then are ye bastards, and not sons.

Do you want to be considered a son or a bastard? You must realize that you are really spirit to claim that you are a son of the Spirit. God only corrects His sons. If you are not spirit, then you are not of Him. You are a bastard child.

v. 9 Furthermore, we have had fathers of our flesh which corrected us, and we gave them reverence: shall we not much rather be in subjection unto the Father of spirits, and live?

We will subject ourselves to correction with reverence from our natural fathers and will obey them, usually. Our natural fathers do not have the power to allow us to live and breathe. If we are truly spirit, the only one that has the power to give us full life here and now is our only father, God.

Heb. 12:10 For they verily for a few days chastened us after their own pleasure; but he for our profit, that we might be partakers of his holiness.

God chastens us not because it pleases Him, but, for our profit or gain. Why? For us to be partakers of His holiness. Now that we have realized that we and God are spirit, we should also realize that we must read and understand God's word by the spirit. We cannot continue to read and interpret it with a carnal mind or by the traditions of men. Carnal understanding cannot begin to grasp what God wants to show us. Adam saw it. Enoch and Elijah experienced a portion of it. Even Moses got a glimpse of it. The apostles saw it. John wrote it down and was told to seal it for the right time. We need to stop looking for some day to come and know that day is here. The time is now. I don't want to just see what those before me saw; I want to experience it in its fullness. What did they see? I hope to show you in the chapters to come.

LET' S REVIEW:

Please take the time to answer these questions. By doing so, it will give you an idea if you retained what you read and help what you read to take root in your spirit.

1. What does *John 4:24* say God is?

2. How must *YOU* worship God?

3. Why have we misunderstood God?

4. *1 Tim.* says God is what?

5. What does 'eternal' mean?

6. What does 'immortal' mean?

7. What does 'invisible' mean?

8. What does 'God' mean?

9. What does 'magistrate' mean?

10. Name some of the effects we see of God.

11. Of what are our bodies made?

12. What will return to God?

13. Did it specifically say any particular spirit?

14. Who gave the spirit?

15. What are the two bodies?

16. What does 'chasteneth' mean?

17. Who does God chasten?

18. Who does God not chasten?

19. Which are you?

20. What does 'endure' mean?

21. Do you endure the chastening or do you run?

22. List some of the chastening that is going on in your life.

23. What must you be to claim you are a son of the Spirit?

24. To whom must we be in subjection to live?

25. Who benefits from the chastening?

26. What will we profit?

27. How must God's word be read and understood?

28. How must we stop reading and interpreting it?

29. What is enmity with God?

30. What is God?

31. What is man?

NOTES:

† Chapter 2 †

Types and Shadows

*Mark 4:11 And he said unto them, Unto you it is given to know the **mystery** of the kingdom of God: but unto them that are without, all these things are done in parables:*

Ephes. 3:9 And to make all men see what is the fellowship of the mystery, which from the beginning of the world hath been hid in God, who created all things by Jesus Christ:

*Col 1:26-27 Even the **mystery** which hath been hid from ages and from generations, but now is made manifest to his saints: To whom God would make known what is the riches of the glory of this **mystery** among the Gentiles; which is Christ in you, the hope of glory:*

There has been a mystery reserved and hidden from mankind from the foundation of the world. It was reserved for a specific generation and was to be revealed and manifested through the life of Jesus and what He accomplished at the cross.

How are we to know the ***mystery?*** It is revealed to us by the Spirit. How do you solve a mystery? First, you have to be made aware that there is a mystery to be solved. Secondly, you begin looking for clues. As you find the clues, the mystery begins to unravel. As it unravels, you begin to see a 'picture' that you had not seen before.

You say, "It was right in front of my eyes all the time and I couldn't see it." We have been so accustomed to man filling us up with doctrine, that we haven't bothered solving the mystery for ourselves. Even detectives get in such a rut solving a crime that they miss very important evidence that was there all the time staring them in the face.

By supplying us with clues and the Holy Spirit to direct us, God has given us the means to unravel the mysteries of His plan and purpose for mankind. It has been reserved for a time and season; a specific generation through whom the fullness of Christ will be manifested. Some of these clues are known as types and shadows or symbolism. The Bible is full of them.

Types and shadows are something natural used to express something spiritual. God is spirit; we are carnal. In order for Him to communicate with us, God uses something natural with which we are familiar to relate something spiritual to us. He also uses similes and allegories. A *simile* is a figure of speech in which one thing is likened to another. Jesus was always likening the Kingdom of God to something.

An *allegory* is a story in which people, things, and events have a symbolic meaning, often instructive. You must put off the old mind set of the religious teachings of men and find for yourself, the teachings of God. This is what Paul constantly told the people in his writings.

2 Cor. 4:18 While we look not at the things which are seen, but at the things which are not seen: for the things which are seen are temporal; but the things which are not seen are eternal.

Heb. 8:5 Who serve unto the example and shadow of heavenly things, as Moses was admonished of God when he was about to make the tabernacle: for, See, saith he, that thou make all things according to the pattern shewed to thee in the mount.

Heb. 9:23-24 It was therefore necessary that the patterns of things in the heavens should be purified with these; but the heavenly things themselves with better sacrifices than these. For Christ is not entered into the holy places made with hands, which are the figures of the true; but into heaven itself, now to appear in the presence of God for us:

Below are some examples of types and shadows. Can you add to the list? Look up scripture for them. Some are given for you.

1. CLOUDS: *2 Peter 2:17; Heb. 12:1; Jude 1:12; Prov. 25:14; Eze. 38:16.* God appeared in a cloud all through the Old Testament as a type and shadow showing us that he would appear in us, His clouds. Yes, clouds are symbolic of **people**.

2. RIGHT HAND: *Ex. 15:6; Mark 14:62.* The right hand represents the **power of God**.

3. LEFT HAND: *Lev. 14:15; Judges 3:21; Jonah 4:11; Matt. 6:3, 25:41.* The left hand speaks of the **power of man**.

4. HORSE: *Job 39:19; Psalm 33:17; 147:10.* A horse was the most powerful thing they knew in their day. The color of the horse determined the kind of power it represented.

5. RED: *Gen. 25:25; Ex. 25:5; Num. 21:4; Deut. 1:40; Josh. 24:6; Isa. 1:18; 11:2; Est. 1:6.* Red represents two things. Adam means ruddy or red, human being. Red, depending on how it is being

used, can represent the **Adamic Nature** or, if referring to one of the seven spirits of God, **Understanding**.

6. WHITE: PURITY, RIGHTEOUSNESS, SPIRIT OF THE LORD

7. GREEN = KNOWLEDGE, LIFE

8. BLUE = MIGHT AND POWER

9. YELLOW = WISDOM

10. PURPLE = FEAR OF THE LORD

11. ORANGE = COUNSEL

12. GOLD = DEITY

13. BLACK = DARKNESS, EVIL

14. BROWN = EARTHY NATURE

15. PALE = DEATH

16. BLOOD = LIFE

17. TREE = PEOPLE, CULT, RELIGION

18. FIRE = GOD'S PRESENCE, JUDGMENT

19. OIL = HOLY SPIRIT, ANOINTING

20. LEAVEN = DECAY AND SPIRITUAL CORRUPTION

21. BREAD = THE WORD, NOURISHMENT

22. KINGDOM = REALM OF RULERSHIP

23. FACE = DIRECTION YOU ARE HEADED

24. CORN = WORD TO FEED

25. SUN = JESUS

26. WOMAN = CHURCH OR SOULISH NATURE

27. DRAGON = DEVIL OR EVIL INFLUENCE

28. HELL = REALM OF THE DEAD, UNSEEN, GRAVE

29. TRUMPET = SOUND OR VOICE OF INFLUENCE

30. RAIN = SPIRITUAL BLESSINGS

31. SHEEP = GOD'S PEOPLE

32. EARTH = CARNAL MAN

33. ROOT = BEING ESTABLISHED IN SOMETHING

34. HEART = MIND

35. SILVER = REDEMPTION

36. LIGHT = KNOWLEDGE, HEAVENLY

37. SCARLET = SUFFERING AND SACRIFICE

38. IRON = STRENGTH

39. BRASS = JUDGMENT AND JUSTICE

40. EGYPT = BONDAGE, SIN AND WORLD

41. JERICHO = WORLD

42. KADESH-BARNEA = PLACE OF DECISION

43. CANAAN = SPIRIT FILLED LIVING

44. WOOD, HAY, STUBBLE = HUMANITY

45. PASSOVER = DEATH OF CHRIST, FIRST STEP OF SALVATION

46. LEPROSY = TYPE OF SIN

47. WATER = SPIRIT

48. SALT = PRESERVE; ABILITY TO AVOID ERROR OR DANGER

49. MOUNTAIN = HIGH PLACE

50. FEET = DIRECTION, FOUNDATION

51. OXEN = 12 APOSTLES, MINISTERS OF THE WORD

52. STAR = INDIVIDUAL MINISTRY

53. MOON = CHURCH

54. MAN = SPIRIT OVER SOUL

55. SEA = MULTITUDES OR WORLD

56. GRAVE = MEMORY/MEMORIAL

57. FIELD = WORLD

58. STONE = SEED

59. GOAT = REBELLIOUS NATURE

60. ANGEL = MESSAGE OR MESSENGER, PREACHER

61. TEMPLE = BODY

62. HAIR = GLORY

63. BED = PLACE OF SPIRITUAL OR CARNAL CONCEPTION

64. BOTTOMLESS PIT = NO FOUNDATION; MAN'S MIND OR IMAGINATION

65. KINGS OF THE EAST = EASTERN PHILOSOPHY

66. HEAVEN = GOD AND HIS DOMAIN, SPIRITUAL REALM OR SPIRITUAL MIND

67. FIG TREE = ISRAELITES

68. ARK OF THE COVENANT = GOD'S WORD

69. FLESH = CARNAL NATURE

70. LAZARETH = CHRIST

71. LAMB = CHRIST

72. -ITES = UNGODLY NATURES IN MAN

73. ARK = BODY, SOUL, SPIRIT; SAFE PLACE IN CHRIST

74. MANSION = PEOPLE

75. HOUSE = FAMILY MEMBERS IN HOUSEHOLD, BODY

76. NAME = NATURE, CHARACTERISTICS

77. HORN = SOUND, VOICE OF INFLUENCE

78. BEAST = NATURE OF MAN WITHOUT GOD

79. JORDAN = DEATH

Another deciphering tool God has given us is the code of numbers. This can be proven all through the Bible. *Example: Forty - Trials, Probation, and Testings.* How many years did the Israelites wander around in the wilderness and why? How many days was Jesus in the wilderness and why? How many days did it rain? How long was Moses on the mount? Find scriptures to prove the following:

ONE: Unity

TWO: Union, Division, Witnessing

THREE: Resurrection, Divine Completeness and Perfection

FOUR: Creation --- World

FIVE: Grace or God's Goodness

SIX: Weakness of Man - Evils of Satan - Manifestation of Sin

SEVEN: Completeness - Spiritual Perfection

EIGHT: New Birth, New Creation or New Beginning

NINE: Fruit of Spirit - Divine Completeness From the Lord

TEN: Testimony - Law and Responsibility

ELEVEN: Judgment and Disorder

TWELVE: Governmental Perfection

THIRTEEN: Depravity and Rebellion

FOURTEEN: Deliverance or Salvation

FIFTEEN: Rest

SIXTEEN: Love

SEVENTEEN: Victory

EIGHTEEN: Bondage

NINETEEN: Faith

TWENTY: Redemption

TWENTY-ONE: Exceeding Sinfulness of Sin

TWENTY-TWO: Light

TWENTY-THREE: Death

TWENTY-FOUR: The Priesthood

TWENTY-FIVE: The Forgiveness of Sins

TWENTY-SIX: The Gospel of Christ

TWENTY-SEVEN: Preaching of the Gospel

TWENTY-EIGHT: Eternal Life

TWENTY-NINE: Departure

THIRTY: The Blood of Christ - Dedications

THIRTY-ONE: Offspring

THIRTY-TWO: Covenant

THIRTY-THREE: Promise

THIRTY-FOUR: Naming of A Son

THIRTY-FIVE: Hope

THIRTY-SIX: Enemy

THIRTY-SEVEN: The Word of God

THIRTY-EIGHT: Slavery

THIRTY-NINE: Disease

FORTY: Trials, Probation and Testings

FORTY-TWO: Israel's Oppression -- Lord's Advent

FORTY-FIVE: Preservation

FIFTY: Holy Spirit

SIXTY: Pride

SIXTY-SIX: Idol Worship

SEVENTY: Universality -- Israel and Her Restoration

ONE HUNDRED: God's Election of Grace -- Children of Promise

ONE HUNDRED NINETEEN: The Resurrection Day—Lord's Day

ONE HUNDRED TWENTY: Divine Period of Probation

ONE HUNDRED FORTY-FOUR: The Spirit Guided Life

ONE HUNDRED FIFTY-THREE: Fruit-Bearing

TWO HUNDRED: Insufficiency

SIX HUNDRED: Warfare

SIX HUNDRED SIXTY-SIX: The Number of The Beast -- Anti-Christ

EIGHT HUNDRED EIGHTY-EIGHT: The First Resurrection Saints

THOUSAND: Divine Completeness and The Glory of God

Using the number chart and types and shadows key given you, decipher the following verse (not according to what you were taught):

Rev. 6:8 And I looked, and behold a <u>pale</u> <u>horse</u>: and his <u>name</u> that sat on him was Death, and <u>Hell</u> followed with him. And power was given unto them over the <u>fourth</u> part of the <u>earth</u>, to kill with sword, and with hunger, and with death, and with the <u>beasts</u> of the earth.

Pale: Horse:

Name: Hell:

Four(th):   Earth:

Beasts:

Where does death take you?

What is man, without God, doing to creation?

Man wants to blame God for all the famines, killings, perversion, etc., but who is truly to blame?

Jesus said in *Rev. 1:18* that He has the keys of hell and of death. He also gave the power of these keys to Peter in *Matt. 16:18-19*. If we are *in Christ*, we have the keys to that same power over death, be it spiritual or physical. Are we using those keys? Are you?

According to *Rev.*, from what is creation dying and why?

John 14:1-4 Let not your <u>heart</u> be troubled: ye believe in God, believe also in me. In my Father's <u>house</u> are many <u>mansions</u>: if it were not so, I would have told you. I go to prepare a place for you. And if I go and prepare a place for you, I will come again, and receive you unto myself; that where I am, there ye may be also. And whither I go ye know, and the way ye know.

Heart: House: Mansions:

Heb. 11 is known as the chapter of the members of the Household of Faith. If we have been reborn, we are a member of the household of faith. Look at this literally. Think of putting mansions, which we to know to be from 4,000 sq. ft. and up, into a house of which we consider to be between 900 and 2,000 sq. ft. If you take God literally and try to make His word literal, then this is not feasible nor possible. It has to be understood spiritually and done spiritually.

If Jesus went away as spirit and returned as spirit and you received him, where did you receive him and where does he abide?

If you are that mansion in His house(hold), then He prepared a place in your spirit where you could receive Him and He could abide with you. How do you know this? Because you know He is the Way, the Truth, and the Life and you have to go through Him to get to the Father.

In *Matt. 23*, Jesus is dealing with the priesthood of that day. He referred to them (simile) as *whited sepulchers* outward, but within, full of dead men's bones. What did He mean by this?

Matt. 24:42-44 Jesus is using an allegory to show them a picture of what?

I pray that as you continue this study, you lay down the old teachings and let God reveal afresh to you His plan and purpose. I pray you begin to see the *Word* in a fresh, new light by the Spirit.

Romans 12:1-2: ...but be ye transformed (changed) by the renewing of your mind, that ye may prove what is good, and acceptable, and perfect, will of God.

NOTES:

† *Chapter 3* †

Seven Days of Creation

Hopefully, after thoroughly studying and completing the last chapter, you have realized that, by using types and shadows, the Bible gives us a complete picture of what God's plan and purpose is for mankind.

If you ever went to school in your lifetime, you surely had to write a research paper. There were specific steps to follow when preparing to write one.

A. First, you do research on the subject. This is where man has become so lazy. Let the preacher tell us; and, they have. They have told us what was told them and what was handed down from generation to generation. We know how our thoughts and opinions are injected into a story we are sharing. We must understand that God was dealing with an eastern culture; thus, He had to use their customs to relate His Word. The western world has a totally different custom. We have tried to fit a square peg into a round hole. It won't fit!

Example: *Deut. 22:5 The woman shall not wear that which pertaineth unto a man, neither shall a man put on a woman's garment: for all that do so are abomination unto the Lord thy God.*

I was taught, through my denomination, that women were not to wear pants. It wasn't until I began to study the manners and customs of the eastern nation that men didn't wear pants, as we know them. Men wore short tunics without under garments. If they had to do strenuous activities, they would pull the back hem between the legs and gird it to the waist with a rope like belt; thus, *gird up your loins.* It is understandable why women were not to wear short tunics without under garments. Imagine the riot!

Let's take a look at this spiritually by using what we have previously learned. If the man represents the spirit and the woman represents the soulish nature, the soul is not to try to move in the spirit realm nor usurp authority over it. It doesn't belong there. It defiles the spirit; thus, produces death. The spirit is not to move in the soulish realm. It would be giving life to the soulish realm. *Flesh and blood cannot inherit ….* The carnality of man cannot enter into the Kingdom or spiritual realm of God.

B. Next, you outline the topic. An outline gives you the general plan or systematic summary of the subject. The first chapter of *Genesis* gives you an outline or summary of God's plan for mankind over a Messianic age of time. Each day was likened to seven thousand years. God is not measured by man's time.

2 Peter 3:8 But, beloved, be not ignorant of this one thing, that one day is with the Lord as a thousand years, and a thousand years as one day.

It didn't say it was specifically, down to the letter, a thousand years, but, AS a thousand years. This is giving you a pattern to use. God told us what was or would be accomplished in each Messianic day. For simplicity, I will refer to each of these days as 'a thousand year day.'

The first chapter could also be called the LEAD in a news story. The LEAD is the first paragraph of a news story and it summarizes the important information in the story. The reader should be able to grasp the main idea from the first paragraph. The lead must be able to stand alone. By using the key to types and shadows and being led by the Spirit, you should be able to read chapter one and know God's plan.

C. After the outline is prepared, you are ready to write the paper or body, following the outline. Thus, the rest of the Bible. The rest of the Bible gives us a more detailed account of what happened in each of the days.

The first sentence of the body is called a *thesis sentence*, which states the main idea of the paper. You will find God's thesis sentence in the second chapter of *Genesis*.

Gen. 2:4-5 These are the generations of the heavens and of the earth when they were created, in the day that the Lord God made the earth and the heavens, 5) And every plant of the field before it was in the earth, and every herb of the field before it grew: for the Lord God had not caused it to rain upon the earth, and there was not a man to till the ground.

To understand the previous verses, remember, see them by the Spirit and not by natural understanding. Do not take them literally. Notice, 'heavens' is plural and 'earth' is singular. During the spiritual evolution of mankind, he has had many 'heavens' or concepts of God. As God reveals more of Himself to mankind, man's 'heavens' or spiritual understanding of God changes; their heavens are shaken.

The earth is our carnality. We have tried to perceive God and His plan with a carnal mind; but, *Romans 8:7* says that the carnal mind is enmity with God.

Genesis 2:4, therefore, states that we are going to read about the generations or lineage of man's spiritual processing. The book of *Job* alone gives you a picture of everything man has to experience to **KNOW** God in His fullness.

Chapter one of *Genesis* contains an overwhelming amount of spiritual insight. Due to time and space, I will not be able to go into great depth; but, I will try to hit the highlights and leave some for you to discover.

The diagram on the next page represents the seven thousand year days and who opened and closed each day. If you will study church history, it will bear this out.

We know our 24 hour day to begin with the morning and end with the evening. In *Gen. 1*, we see that each day began with the evening and ended with the morning. Why? Remember, God used the Jewish customs to reveal His word to them. Each thousand year day began in spiritual darkness, or not knowing God's plan, and ended in spiritual light, or His plan revealed. I have covered the first chapter in outline form.

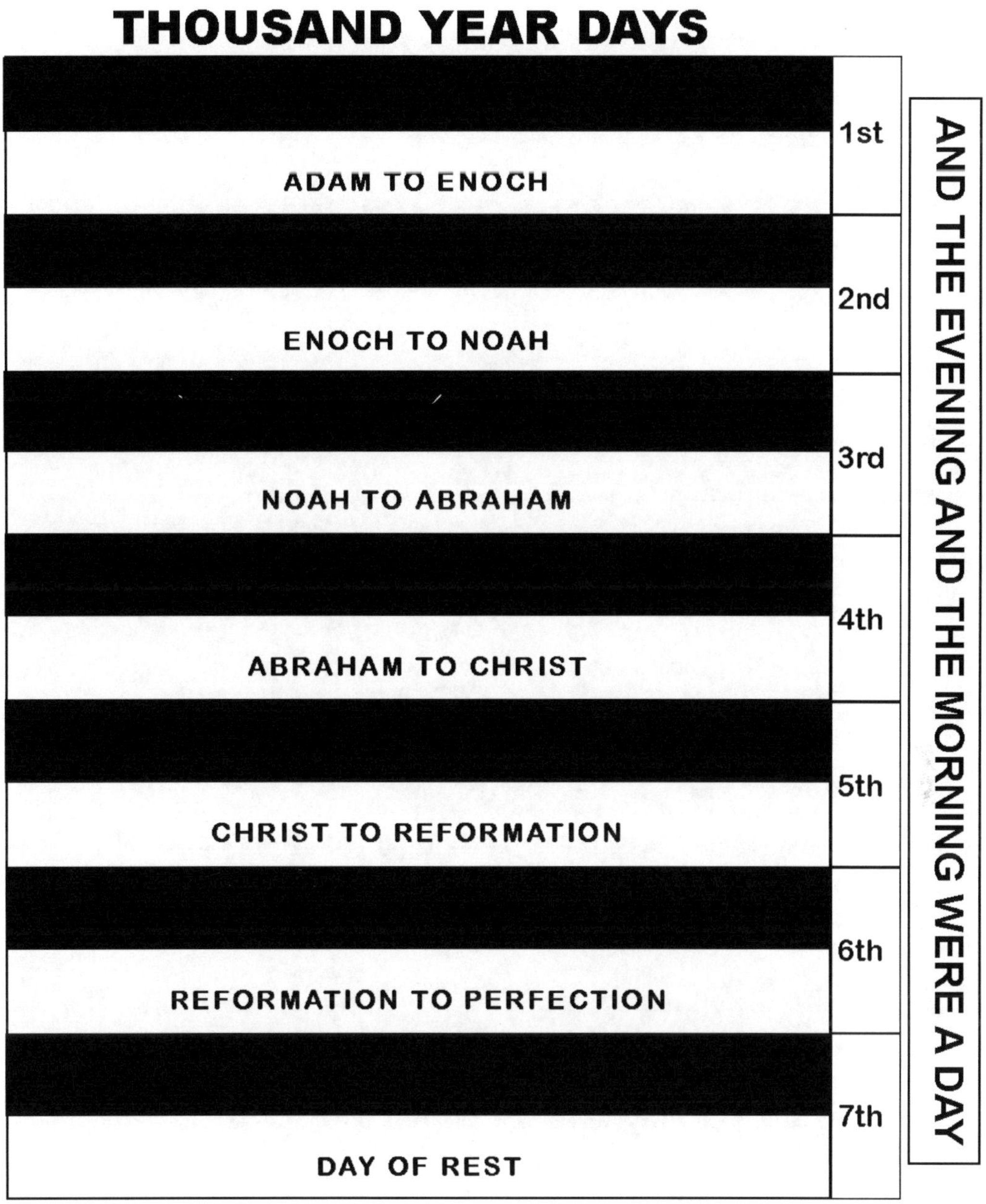

THOUSAND YEAR DAYS

ADAM TO ENOCH	1st
ENOCH TO NOAH	2nd
NOAH TO ABRAHAM	3rd
ABRAHAM TO CHRIST	4th
CHRIST TO REFORMATION	5th
REFORMATION TO PERFECTION	6th
DAY OF REST	7th

AND THE EVENING AND THE MORNING WERE A DAY

Diagram 1: Seven Days of Creation Chart

SEVEN DAYS OF CREATION

1. Introduction:

A. Natural things are patterns of real heavenly things. *Heb. 9: 23-24*

B. Old Testament examples given for our admonition. *1 Cor. 10: 10-11*

C. OT sets pattern for direction not finished product. Join together the pieces and you see a finished garment.

D. OT pattern fit together produced finished product, ***physical manifestation of a Spiritual God*** unto an earthy man. OT was ***Father concealed***, NT is ***Father revealed***.

E. *Gen. 1* is seven day pattern of God's finished will manifested to all creation.

F. *1 Peter 3:8:* One day with the Lord is as a thousand years.

G. God accomplishes something in each thousand year day.

H. Each day begins with the evening and ends with the morning. Each 'day' begins in darkness but ends in light.

2. The First Day: *Gen. 1:1-5:*

A. The earth was without form and void.

   1. First day begins with Adam and ends with Enoch, nearly a thousand years later.

   2. FORM: Hebrew definition - confusion, etc.

   3. VOID: Hebrew definition - to be empty, etc. ***FORM AND VOID - CONFUSED AND EMPTY***.

   4. God took a part of the earth, higher dust, that was without spiritual knowledge of God, and made a creation called 'man.' The Bible is the inspired history of man from the time God begins to deal with man to the time God will ADVANCE him into the MEASURE and STATURE of the FULNESS OF CHRIST: Seven thousand year period of time. *Eph. 4:7; Eph. 4:13.*

   5. *Dan. 4:10-19:* The dream also explains the fall of Adam and results of that fall. Pre - Adamic man did not know God. He was ***without form and void, confused and empty.*** He was the highest form of the dust of the earth. *Prov. 8:26.*

   6. FORMED in Hebrew means to squeeze into shape or form a resolution. Something is molded from an existing substance. CREATE means something comes into being out of nothing. God FORMED the first man Adam. He chose the higher dust of the world, (pre-Adamic man) and squeezed him into shape through a resolution. God

had purposed in himself to make or advance man into His own likeness and image (spirit) and give him dominion. Dominion over what? Dominion over his own will and nature by the spirit and to subdue them. God breathed the spirit of life into the pre-Adamic man, gave him the capacity to communicate with Him on a spiritual plane.

B. Spirit of God moved, and God said, "Let there be light."

1. Believers are called Sons of Light. God reveals Himself to man by preparing them as organs of light, as an eye receives light to see; *Luke 11:34-36.* Adam became Son of Light. The word 'Lucifer' means morning star and *Isa. 14:12* refers to him as being the 'son of the morning.' If you read the entire chapter, before and after, Lucifer is literally referring to the Prince of Persia. Adam was a son of God, he wasn't the begotten son. Adam received the perfect substance: intellect, will, emotion, conscious and subconscious mind of God. He walked in life and did not die; *Gen. 3:22.*

2. His eyes were opened through disobedience and an invisible veil was cast over the Godly spirit within him. Adam begins to see through a glass darkly. He falls from spiritual consciousness into an earthy awareness.

3. Adam fell into condemnation, resulting in death. Why? His (spiritual) eyes were opened. Hebrew for eye: fountain, landscape. He saw what he was before. Adam saw the plan and purpose of God, found himself *spiritually* naked, and condemned himself. *Eph. 1:9-11.*

4. Adam was only a figure or pattern of Him who was to come, Jesus Christ. I view the Adamic race as God's first ministers in the earth. He was of the Melchizedek priesthood.

C. God divided the light from the darkness.

1. Many religious beliefs existed in the days of the Adamic race. According to the *Kettle's Theological Dictionary of the New Testament*, SACHAN was the most significant religion. It was located in the City of Der, in ancient Babylon. Their symbol was a burning sun disc surrounded by the symbol of a serpent. It sounded so much like the truth; but, it appealed to their soul.

2. Adam is driven out of the garden and separated from the light of God. If God is spirit, how could Adam be driven from a literal garden away from God? God is omnipresent. Our <u>body</u> is the <u>garden</u> of God or the temple of God. He tells us so all throughout the Word; *1 Cor. 3:16-17.* Adam ministers from remembrance of light. He saw GOOD and saw EVIL. The way he perceived it destroyed him.

3. Purpose of the first day: Let there be light (spiritual knowledge), and let there be a separation of light and darkness (ignorance).

4. God told him that the day he ate of the mixture he would die. It took Adam 930 years to die. *Gen. 5:5.*

D. Enoch fulfills the first day by losing his identity and becoming the fullness of light. As Adam began the first day in darkness, and sees light (which brings condemnation and death), Enoch finishes the day in light or fulfilling God's plan for that day. He then ushers in the second day. *Heb. 11:5.*

3. The Second Day: *Gen. 1:6-8.*

A. God created the firmament called Heaven.

1. Enoch saw what Adam saw, but by faith, he did not see himself dead in Adam. He saw himself resurrected in Christ. Enoch looked all the way to the end and saw what would be accomplished in Christ. It wasn't by coincidence that he was the seventh generation from Adam. His testimony before he was translated or changed was that he PLEASED God.

2. The second day begins with Enoch and ends with Noah.

3. The word *heaven* was a word coined by the Hebrews to describe God. God describes His nature to Moses in the burning bush as 'I AM' or SELF EXISTENT ONE. (NAME means nature or character).

4. Jesus declared Himself as 'I AM.' *John 8:58.*

5. *Gen. 6:1-2:* Two classes of people, **sons of God and daughters of men.** After Enoch's translation, the earth was filled with sons of God (Adamic race), and daughters of men (seedline of the beasts of the field, those that did not know God).

6. Methuselah, son of Enoch, means *IT SHALL BE SENT OR DELUGE.* Enoch named his son as a prophecy to creation as a witness to what was coming: The flood or deluge. It would destroy all fleshly identity.

7. Methuselah lived 969 years as a witness in the earth; but, mankind was looking backward and missed the day of their deliverance in the ark.

8. Enoch is referred to as 'the seventh from Adam.' Being the light in his day, he was not limited, but, could see the end from the beginning and lived accordingly. The (knowledge) light of his revelation was translated out of the first day into the seventh day. (Remember, the ministry of Elijah showed up in John's day). Enoch's revelation was a word of LIFE. He embraced it, and by faith, experienced it. Enoch did not experience death, literally or spiritually.

9. Noah finds grace in the eyes of God. Noah is informed of God's plan to send rain upon the earth and is given blue prints to build the ark that would become his salvation. If you study the ark, you can again see God's plan for man. Noah remembers the witness of Methuselah and obeys God's will for the second day. Remember, it had never rained before. Dew had come from the earth to water the ground. Look for the spiritual picture. This is not natural rain or natural earth.

B. God commanded the firmament to be a division between the waters above and the waters below.

1. Sons of God surrendered to the mixture of knowledge that

their forefather, Adam, partook of and began to mingle with other religions. (How many of you, through marriage, have changed your doctrine or church affiliation?) There had to be a separation in order to preserve a seed line.

2. The ark was to become a refuge; but, God also commanded it to be a division between the waters that fell from above and the waters that rose from beneath. Noah enters the ark. God caused the rain to fall from above and waters to rise from beneath. The ark becomes the firmament between the two waters.

3. The ark was a type and shadow of God's plan of salvation for man that will separate the sons of God from the daughters of men. Light from darkness and flesh from Spirit.

4. The Third Day: *Gen. 1:9-13.*

A. Commanded the waters to be gathered into one place.

1. The Third Day begins with Noah and ends with Abraham. Noah entered into the ark on the 17th day of the 2nd month.

2. The #2 means: unity, division, and witnessing. By uniting with God's word, he entered in and found safety. There was a division from the waters beneath and waters above by the ark. There was a witness that Noah had heard the word of the Lord when the waters fell and destroyed all flesh in the world as they knew it.

3. The #17 means victory. Noah became victorious when, by faith, he brought the invisible into the visible by building the ark and supplying a place of safety or salvation.

4. *Gen. 11:1-14.* In one mind and one accord, we find the spirit of the people or the waters gathered together to build a tower to heaven to make a name for themselves, Babel (confusion). They were following after an order Noah had established not God. God had completed his purpose for the second day through Noah and was bringing in the third day. He, therefore, confounded their language and scattered them abroad.

B. Let dry land appear.

1. Noah was God's new earth. He built an altar and offered up burnt offerings to the Lord. God gave Noah a promise that He would not curse the ground again for man's sake nor smite again all living things.

C. Let the earth bring forth.

1. *Gen. 9:1.* Even though Noah found grace in the eyes of the Lord, in *Gen. 9:20,* we see Noah's weakness in the flesh. He planted a vineyard, drank the wine, and was drunken, and was uncovered within his tent. This is spiritual.

2. God intended for the order of the day to be changed; but, like his forefather, Adam, Noah became a husbandman tilling the ground. He brought another day through the flood with him. Noah exalted himself instead of God to the extent that he became drunken on the fruit of his labor

(coming through the flood), and like Adam, awakened to find himself naked or not clothed with God.

3. *Gen. 12:1-3.* God calls Abram out of his father's house and tells him He will make his name great (contrary to the tower of Babel). God does not want us to achieve greatness by our own works or ideas. God promised Abram that his seed would be as the sand of the sea and the stars in multitude; and, he would be the father of many nations. Abram was to be the earth that would bring forth seed within itself.

4. Abram doubted God when He promised him a seed. Living under the code of Hammurabi, Sarah and Abram decided to give God a helping hand. Sarah gave Abram her hand maiden, Hagar, who produced Ishmael (flesh). Hagar despised Sarah and Abram had to choose between the two. God told Abram to cast out Hagar and her son. Abram was distraught, thinking he was casting out his seed line. Ishmael was fruit of Abram's earth, but, he was not from the married wife. God made provision for the bond woman and her son or the carnal or soulish nature of man.

5. Isaac is born and becomes the promised seed line that would fulfill the commandment for the third day: Let the earth bring forth the seed within itself. The seed of Abraham became God's chosen race. Abram became Abraham, from **high father** to **father of a multitude.**

6. The seed of Abraham, children of Israel, came into being through a manifestation of faith, yet, did not enter into the promises of God because of their unbelief.

5. The Fourth Day: *Gen. 1:14-18.*

A. Set lights in the firmament of heaven to give light upon the earth.

1. The fourth day begins with Abraham and ends with Jesus. The promise of a seed line was not the natural nation of Israel, but, the seed line of Christ.

2. The Israelites were ruled by the Levitical priesthood. It became a corrupt priesthood, but, God raised up Samuel to minister in the priest's office. The people were not content to be ruled by God and wanted a king. Samuel was sent to anoint David.

3. David was given the same promise as Abraham: "When thy days be fulfilled, and thou sleep with thy fathers, I will set up thy seed after thee, which shall proceed out of thy bowels; and, I will establish the throne of his kingdom forever."

4. *Psa. 16:8-11.* David knew that God was not referring to a natural kingdom. He was resting in hope that his flesh or seed not see corruption. He is speaking of Jesus. All through the scriptures Jesus is called the son of David because He was born from the lineage of David.

5. Malachi prophesies his coming in *Mal. 4:2.*

6. *John 1:4-5; 1:9; 8:12.* These scriptures show that Jesus was that light created in the fourth day.

7. Mankind walked in spiritual darkness when the light went out in Adam. The power of life and death was taken from man and given to Satan. Because of the absence of light

from Adam to Moses, death reigned. Being only a shadow of the reality, the Mosaic Law brought more death through condemnation.

8. *Luke 10:18.* Jesus said He beheld Satan fall as lightning from heaven. Why? Because, when Jesus fulfilled the law and became the perfect sacrifice, He cleansed the heavens. Jesus destroyed the one who had the power of death, the devil. *Destroyed* means: render inactive. Jesus rendered the devil inactive in His humanity. "The prince of this world cometh, but hath no part in me."

9. *Prov. 18:21.* The power of life and death has been given back to man.

10. Jesus was the light of the world; the sun of righteousness established in the heavens that has arisen and dispelled the darkness of the past, present, and future.

B. To divide the day from the night.

1. *2 Sam. 22:29; Isa. 42:16; 1 Thes. 5:4-5; 2 Peter 1:19.* The Day Star is Christ, who is to rule over us. The wise men who saw the star in the east recognized it as being His star. Not everyone saw it. People are looking for Jesus to return in the flesh; but, He said, 'Know me no more after the flesh.' He is that Day Star that is rising in our hearts. If you follow that star, you will find Him. Stop looking upward in the sky for a physical manifestation and start looking inward for one.

2. The lesser light in the natural heavens is the moon. It has no light of its own and can only reflect the light of the sun.

Hence, the moon represents the church which hasn't a light of its own, but, reflects the light Christ. Multitudes are still catching only a portion of the light and are still living in darkness. There are some who are living in the consciousness of the day. Their night has passed and the darkness that covered the deep has been dispelled.

3. *1 Cor. 13:9-10.*

C. Made the stars also.

1. Stars are God's individual ministries. They, too, must reflect the light of the sun (son).

2. *Jude 1:13.* Men are referred to as wandering stars. *Rev. 8:12.* They fell from a spiritual realm of ministry into an earthy one. *Isa. 30:26.*

3. David began the Fourth Day and Jesus Christ, the seed of David, fulfilled it and became the great light (sun), established the church (moon), and called a ministry (stars) to reflect His light in the earth.

4. The light of the moon shall be as the light of the sun. There will be a time when the church will no longer shine in part, but, will shine as bright as the sun. When this happens, the light of the sun will be as the light of seven full days (seven thousand years) of knowledge. His full purpose will be revealed, nothing hidden. We now have seen the light of six days and the seventh day is upon us.

5. God is binding up the breach of His people, healing the stroke of their wound: The mind of mankind.

5. The Fifth Day: *Gen. 1:20-23.*

1. Jesus came at the end of the Fourth Day as the Way, the Truth, and the Life. The Fifth Day begins with Christ and ends with the reformation of Martin Luther: The just shall live by faith.

2. Life came out of the waters. What do the waters represent? *Joel 2:23.* The former and latter rains fell within the year. The former to germinate the crops and cause them to grow; the latter to mature them for harvest. Over two thousand years ago, The Holy Ghost fell during the Feast of Pentecost. This was the former rain or teaching rain. When it fell on those in the upper room, it watered the word Jesus had planted in them and caused it to come alive and grow. The early church was established on the word watered by this rain.

3. The early church was destined to pass away. *Rev. 13:1.* Sea represents multitudes of humanity. Seven heads were seven nations that had ruled over the nation of Israel: Babylon, Media, Persia, Greece, Egypt, Syria, Rome. Ten horns - ten voices of influence. When Alexander the Great died, Greece was divided among his four generals, making ten voices. These influences caused them to become an adulterous generation. They began to worship other gods.

4. Dragon - Satan; Red Dragon - Red means Adam in Hebrew or can be referring to the nation of Israel moving under the influence of the Adamic nature.

5. *Eze. 47:1, 3.* The doctrine of Christ came from the eastern

world. The tribe of Judah camped on the east side of the tabernacle. He was the sun (son) of righteousness that rose from the east. The waters (spirit) began to flow and were measured. The early church received a truth. This truth was tried and stood in the wilderness experience. It stood in measure to the ankles. It became the foundation of the church. The feet and ankles support the rest of the body.

6. After the persecution of the early church during the dark ages, Christianity was brought to its knees under the burden of the Roman rule.

7. The loins is the reproductive area. When the reformation took place, the church once again began to multiply and produce after the spirit. The waters to swim in are for the Sixth Day.

6. The Sixth Day: *Gen. 1:26-31.*

A. Let the earth bring forth living creatures after their kind.

1. At the end of the Fifth Day, the water has risen to the loins. The church multiplies over the next 1000 years. In 1948, the latter rain fell upon all flesh. *Joel 2:28-32.* The sun was darkened in the Fifth Day by the fleshly rule of Rome. Their only link to God was through Papacy. We see the Sixth Day beginning with the reformation of the church and ends with us, today.

2. *Gen. 1:24-31.* Man has two natures: Adamic (carnal) and spiritual.   These two natures war against each other con-

stantly for rulership in this earth (body). *Gal. 5:17-22; 1 Cor. 3:1-3; Rom. 8:13.* God's command was 'Let the earth bring forth the living creature that hath life. Since Calvary, God's people, although they have the life of Christ within, have been bringing forth the fruit of the earthy creature. They still have the mixture of good and evil in their minds. As a result, their flesh is seeing corruption or dying. It can be likened to having faith with which doubt is mixed. The doubt negates the faith.

3. The spirits of the dead in Christ were made perfect by faith, yet, not perfect without us. Why? Jesus purchased the **whole** man: ***body, soul, and spirit***. Having the spirit made perfect by faith is an in-part salvation. *Romans 8* says the whole world is travailing to be delivered from the bondage of corruption, death. Paul had the first fruits of the spirit, the Holy Ghost; but, even he was groaning within himself to be released from the bondage of death.

4. Job declared: *My flesh shall rest in hope, all the appointed days of my time will I wait till my change come, immortality. 1 Cor. 15:49.*

B. Let the Beast bring forth.

1. The beast nature of man is being brought forth today due to the latter rain. Rain will resurrect every seed; and today, we see every seed that is in man's earth coming to maturity. *2 Peter 2:12; Jude 1:4, 10-12.* All seeds conceived in *Genesis* have gone through conception, gestation time, and now, we are about to see the birth.

C. Let us make man in our likeness and image.

1. *Rom. 5:14.* Adam was a type or shadow of the creation fashioned or created after the image of God. He was formed from the dust of the earth, carnal elements. His thoughts and emotions were formed by his environmental surroundings and lower than that of Spirit. He was an earthy image of the invisible God. God is spirit and man had to be changed to be able to stand as a finished product. He had to be gathered into Spirit or re-birthed.

2. Man had been sentenced to die. Jesus humbled himself unto death. *1 Cor. 15:36; John 12:24.* He paid the price for sin, the perfect sacrifice. That seed in him that was spirit, however, did not see corruption. His divine nature swallowed up all traces of the earthy identity. *1 Cor. 15:45.*

3. *John 1:14. Begotten* means: only-born, sole. Jesus, as the only begotten son of God, had the seed line of the Father in his loins. The power to reproduce after the spirit. *John 5:21.*

4. He was the finished product, the perfect seed line that would produce a new creation of sons, all in the likeness and image of that incorruptible seed. He experienced a change in His flesh or was transfigured and went away in the form of spirit and returned again, as He said He would, 50 days later on the day of Pentecost as spirit. When the Spirit is received by the earthy creation, the earthy will experience a change and will reproduce after its own kind.

5. *1 Cor. 15:53.* What must we put on? Today, 6,000+ years from Adam's day, man will become in the likeness and image of his Father God through the spirit of Christ.

D. Let man have dominion over all the earth.

1. God intended that His creation would rule and reign on the earth. Man was given 6,000 years or six days to rule. In the Seventh Day or the Millennium, God will rule and reign. The kingdoms of this world will become the kingdoms of our Lord and His Christ. The word 'Christ' means anointed. There will be a people on the earth as the in - Christed seed who will take dominion over their flesh. They will be fruit-ful and multiply and replenish the earth after the Spirit.

7. The Seventh Day. *Genesis 2:2-3.*

1. In the Sixth Day, God brought forth a many membered son that was an offspring of the Spirit. On the Seventh Day, God rested.   God does not intend for us to leave the earth, but, to take dominion over it. *Isa. 45:18; Prov. 10: 30; John 17:15.* It's the Christ in you, the hope of glory, that will bring you to the time to see this happen. *Col. 1: 27.* If Jesus Christ has the keys to death and hell, and, if He dwells in us, why would we run from our enemies?

2. *Ex. 31:14-18.* This is a covenant God made with the chil-dren of Israel. The Jews faithfully kept a natural Sabbath and it is a picture for us.

3. *Heb. 9:24; 8:6-10.* This is His plan of a new covenant with better promises. *Col. 2:13-17.*

4. *Psa. 132:4-5.* According to David, God is looking for a habitation, a place to dwell. *Isa. 66:1-2.* God is looking to man for a habitation of rest. *Eph. 2:19-22.* God desires to dwell in mankind in a state of rest. Read *Heb. 3; 4:1-3, 9-12.* God spoke His plan into existence in *Genesis.* It has naturally been fulfilled, now it has to be fulfilled spiritually. *Isa. 28: 9-12; Acts 2:33.* Jesus allowed the Spirit of God to consume Him. Are you willing to allow the Spirit of God to consume you that you may become LIFE on the earth?

I realize that this was a lot to consume with very little depth of explanation. To read about the [1]*Seven Days of Creation* in a greater depth, you may contact:

Alyce McPherson

HC 64, Box 3670

Tuskahoma, OK 74574

She has written an excellent book on this subject, along with other books concerning *Life.*

---

1. <u>Seven Days of Creation;</u> McPherson, Alyce. The information for this chapter was taken from her personal writings by permission.

LET'S REVIEW:

1. The first chapter of *Genesis* gives us an outline or summary of what?

2. According to *2 Peter,* God does not want us to be what? How did he compare His time to man's time?

3. 'Heavens' are man's concepts of what?

4. Why did each day start with the evening and end with the morning?

5. Of what does the book of *Job* give you?

6. To whom does the Old Testament point? What does the New Testament do?

7. Who begins the first day and who ends it?

8. What does the word 'form' mean?

9. What does the word 'void' mean?

10. Together, these two words give us the picture of the condition of what?

11. How did Adam begin the first day? In What did Adam walk?

12. How did Enoch finish it?

13. What are believers called?

14. What does the word 'Lucifer' mean?

15. According to the definition of Lucifer, who would this make him spiritually?

(**Hint:** *John 8:44* says the devil was a murderer from the beginning and a liar and father of lies, so it can't be him. He could not have been a son of light and be a murderer and liar from the beginning.)

16. Where does Adam fall?

17. Adam fell into condemnation, resulting in death. Why?

18. What did he see?

19. How did he find himself?

We've always been taught that God killed an animal and clothed Adam; but, I've yet to find that in the scriptures. However, I can look at myself and see that my spiritual body is clothed with skins.

20. Where is the real garden?

21. What was the purpose of the first day?

22. What caused Enoch to see himself resurrected in Christ?

23. What were the two classes of people in the earth after Enoch's translation?

24. What did Methuselah's name prophesy?

25. What divided the waters below from the waters above?

26. Of what was the ark a type and shadow?

27. How was Noah victorious?

28. What was God's new earth in the Third Day?

29. Adam and Noah made the same mistake. What was it?

30. What did God promise Abram?

31. What did Abram have to do to receive the promise?

32. When Abram produced Ishmael, after what had he produced?

33. Who became the promised seed line to fulfill the Third Day

Commandment?

34. What kept the children of Israel from entering into the promises of God?

Many believers have missed out on their *FULL INHERITANCE* because of this. You can't spend an inheritance after you are dead.

35. Who was David's seed?

36. Light was absent from whom to whom?

37. We see light created again in the Fourth Day. Who was this light?

38. What did the Mosaic Law bring and resulted in what?

39. Who is the Day Star and where is it rising?

40. What doesn't have a light of its own?

41. What are the stars and whose light do they reflect?

42. What is God healing?

43. At the end of the Fourth Day, Jesus came as what?

44. What was Martin Luther's revelation?

45. What were the two rains experienced in the Fifth Day?

46. What was the purpose of the former rain?

47. What was the purpose of the latter rain?

48. When the Holy Ghost fell, it was also known as what rain?

49. What were the seven heads and ten horns mentioned in *Rev. 13:1?*

50. What does the Red Dragon represent?

51. From where did the doctrine of Christ come?

52. How was the sun darkened?

53. What are man's two natures?

54. How were the spirits of the dead in Christ made perfect?

55. What did Jesus purchase?

56. What was brought forth in man due to the latter rain?

57. Who had the power to reproduce after the spirit?

58. According to *1 Cor. 15:53*, what must we put on?

59. How long was man given to rule?

60. What does the word 'Christ' mean?

61. Who was brought forth in the Sixth Day?

62. What does God intend for us to do in the Seventh Day?

63. Where does Christ dwell?

64. Where will God rest?

65. Where will man rest?

66. How will we become LIFE in the earth?

67. Who is to usher in the Seventh Day?

NOTES:

† *Chapter 4* †

The Coming of The Lord

In 1830, a young Scottish lass named Margaret MacDonald from Port Glasgow, Scotland, had a spiritual revelation of the coming of the Lord. Several noted Bible scholars of that day took her thoughts and began to add their views. Among them were Edward Irving of the Catholic Apostolic Church of England and John Darby, founder of the Plymouth Brethren.

Darby visited the United States ministering his version of the revelation. Thus, his teaching of dispensationalism became part of the *Scofield Reference Bible (1909)*. From these notes sprang the new teaching of the rapture in our country. Church history bears out this fact. A spiritual revelation from God had once again been handled and defiled by man, reduced to a carnal and literal thought.

Scholars have used *1 Thessalonians 4:17* on which to base their argument or doctrine. Again, they are forgetting that God is spirit; thus, it must be understood as a spiritual seizing. When I accepted Christ, He 'caught' me up in Him or 'seized' me. I get caught up more and more in Him every day, until He is more my life than this earthy life.

I am being changed daily; line upon line, precept upon precept, from glory to glory. If you study the Bible closely, you will find through it that there are many 'comings' of the Lord to His people.

Let's take a look at the coming that is relevant to our day. Again, keep in mind that the Bible is full of types and shadows to give us a picture of the spiritual truth. You must understand a different concept of 'Heaven' than the concept we have been taught that Heaven was way off out there somewhere. You must understand what a kingdom is and what the Bible says the Kingdom of Heaven is. You must understand where Jesus Christ and His Kingdom really dwells.

Acts 1:9-11 And when he had spoken these things, while they beheld, he was taken up; and a cloud received him out of their sight. And while they looked steadfastly toward heaven as he went up, behold, two men stood by them in white apparel; which also said, Ye men of Galilee, why stand ye gazing up into heaven? this same Jesus, which is taken up from you into heaven, shall so come in like manner as ye have seen him go into heaven.

Because the scripture reads 'a cloud received him', people have taken it literally. If God is spirit, we must read His word spiritually. What form was Jesus in when He went away? Spirit. There-fore, what form will He be in when He comes again? Spirit. When did He come again? Fifty days later on the day of Pentecost to the 120 in the upper room. In what manifestation? The Holy Ghost. Yes, the Holy Ghost and the spirit of Jesus Christ are one and the same.

John 14:6-7 Jesus saith unto him, I am the way, the truth, and the life: no man cometh unto the Father, but by me. If ye had known me, ye should have known my Father also: and from henceforth ye know him, and have seen him.

Our biggest error is viewing the Father, the Son, and the Holy Ghost as three separate personages instead of realizing that they are three different spiritual appearings of God to man.

John 14:13-17 And whatsoever ye shall ask in my name, that will I do, that the Father may be glorified in the Son. If ye shall ask any thing in my name, I will do it. If ye love me, keep my command-ments. And I will pray the Father, and he shall give you another Com-forter, that he may abide with you for ever; Even the <u>Spirit of truth</u>; whom the world cannot receive, because it seeth him not, neither knoweth him: <u>but ye know him</u>; <u>for he dwelleth with you</u>, <u>and shall be IN you.</u>

Who is the Spirit of truth? The above scriptures call both Jesus Christ and The Comforter or Holy Ghost the truth. Since we know there is only one with the truth, we should realize they are one and the same. How could they already know the Comforter? Because, He had already dwelled with them, Jesus. The scripture says they knew Him because The Comforter/Jesus Christ had already dwelled WITH them; and, then He would dwell IN them.

John 14:18 I (Jesus) will not leave you comfortless: I will come to you (The Comforter).

Jesus has told them He would send a comforter and now He says He will not leave them comfortless. Who will come? The Comforter or the Holy Ghost.

John 14: 20-21, 23 At that day ye shall know that I am in my Father, and ye in me, and I in you. (How could He be IN them unless He came again as spirit?) *He that hath my commandments, and keepeth them, he it is that loveth me: and he that loveth me shall be loved of my Father, and I will love him, and will manifest myself to him.*

----- *Jesus answered and said unto him, If a man love me, he will keep my words: and my Father will love him, and we will come unto him, and make our abode with him.* The creative spirit (Father) of God and His word (Christ) will take up their abode (mansion) with you.

John 14:24-26 He that loveth me not keepeth not my sayings: and the word which ye hear is not mine, but the Father's which sent me. These things have I spoken unto you, being yet present with you. But the Comforter, which is the Holy Ghost, whom the Father will send in my name (nature), he shall teach you all things, and bring all things to your remembrance, whatsoever I have said unto you.

John 16:7 Nevertheless I tell you the truth; It is expedient for you that I go away: for if I go not away, the Comforter will not come unto you; but if I depart, I will send him unto you.

Why could the Comforter come only if Jesus went away? Because, Jesus was in flesh and had to leave that form in order to return as Spirit.

Acts 1:2 Until the day in which he was taken up, after that he through the Holy Ghost (or in the form of the Holy Ghost) had given commandments unto the apostles whom he had chosen:

How had Jesus given them commandments?

I hope I have been able to show you through scripture that Jesus Christ did return as the two men said He would in like manner as He went away. They specifically asked 'Why stand ye gazing UP into heaven. They were literally gazing up. The two were telling them not to look for Him literally as they were doing; but, to look for Him spiritually: *this same Jesus* — went away as spirit ... *shall so come in like manner* — returned as spirit.

The -ing suffix on the word 'coming' makes it a progressive word. Jesus came two thousand years ago and has been coming ever since in His body --- believers. We just have not seen Him in His fullness in us yet because He has not arrived at His final destination point -- the fullness of seven days -- which is on us today. We are about to witness the full manifestation of His coming in a people. To understand this, we too, have to understand His Kingdom of Heaven.

KINGDOM OF HEAVEN

When you begin to realize what His Kingdom is and where it is, you will realize and appreciate the 'true' coming of Christ. A kingdom is a realm or domain of rulership. Where does Christ rule? Out of us. Where would this put His domain of rulership? We all agree that God is omnipotent and omnipresent. If He is everywhere, then, what would be the difference of Him in you and Him out in the universe? If He is the same here as there, why not stay here and dwell with Him? What's the need to leave? Forget the tribulation. Scripture proves it has been around from the beginning. God never ran from anything nor will He start. He's omnipotent and sovereign. He rules over *ALL* things!

John 17:15, Jesus prays 'Lord, don't take them out of the world, but keep them from the evil.' We read in *Acts 14:22* that through much tribulation (testings) we will enter into the Kingdom of God. It is going to take tribulation to get us there. If you run from it, you won't enter the Kingdom. *Rom. 5* says tribulation works patience. Hey?!!

Patience is a fruit of the Spirit! We can't have patience without tribulation! *2 Cor. 1:4* tells us that Jesus comforts us in all our tribulation; and, in *John 16:33*, Jesus says that in the world you will have tribulation; but, be of good cheer: He has overcome the WORLD! If we believe that He is in us, then, why run? Face tribulation; deal with it, and win!

Col. 1:13 Who hath delivered us from the power of darkness, and hath translated us into the kingdom of his dear Son:

When we accepted Him as our Savior, we were immediately

transferred into His Kingdom. It didn't say some day we would be translated. 'Hath' is a past-tense word. We, also, need to realize that obtaining full salvation is more than accepting Christ as our savior. This is proven by the three major feasts that the children of Israel were commanded to keep. They could not just celebrate one or two of them. They had to celebrate all three. This will be covered in detail in another book. *2 John 1:8* speaks of receiving a FULL reward. This tells me that you can receive a partial reward. I, for one, do not want to miss out on my FULL reward; therefore, I am searching diligently for it.

Col. 3:4 When Christ, who is our life, shall appear, then shall ye also appear with him in glory.

If He is IN us, as it states in *John 14*, and we are in Him, then, we will be revealed with Him in glory. He will be seen ***THROUGH*** us! We are His ***GLORY!!!***

Matt. 16:28 Verily I say unto you, There be some standing here, which shall not taste of death, till they see the Son of man coming in his kingdom.

Six days later, after Jesus told His apostles this, Peter, James, and John went with Jesus to a high mount and witnessed the SON OF MAN COMING IN HIS KINGDOM. Here, Jesus experienced His change or transfiguration (the one we will experience). By faith, when we accepted Him as our savior, we were spiritually transferred into His Kingdom; but, experientially, we are not there yet. Our soul and body needs to align with the Spirit of Christ in us. David talks about his soul being restored. When Jesus was telling His apostles to go and tell everyone the Kingdom of Heaven was at hand, He was talking about what was about to happen to

Him and what He was about to experience. This experience changed the order of that day. Life was restored.

Rom. 14:17 plainly tells us that the Kingdom of God is not eating and drinking (something tangible); but, righteousness and peace and joy (a condition) (WHERE???) in the Holy Ghost. Where does the Holy Ghost dwell? IN YOU!!!!!!

1 Cor. 4:20 For the Kingdom of God does not consist of words, but in power. (condition)

Eph. 2:19-22 Now therefore ye are no more strangers and foreigners, but fellow citizens with the saints, and of the household of God; And are built upon the foundation of the apostles and prophets, Jesus Christ himself being the chief corner stone; In whom all the building fitly framed together groweth unto a holy temple in the Lord: In whom ye also are builded together for a habitation of God through the Spirit.

<u>We</u> are His dwelling place.

Eph. 3:9 And to make all men see what is the fellowship of the mystery, which from the beginning of the world hath been hid in God, who created all things by Jesus Christ.

There is a mystery that has been hidden through the ages, for a reason I might add; but, it is being brought to light. Look for this mystery.

1 Tim. 6:16 says our Lord dwells in unapproachable light (light or understanding that you can't see with these natural eyes); whom no man *has* seen or *can* see. Quit looking for Him in a single body as He once was and start looking for Him in a many-membered body (*1 Cor 12:12, 27*). When you still confine Him to a man Jesus returning, you are limiting His powers and awesomeness! If He was going to set up a Kingdom as one man, He would have done it the first time.

Look around and inside. He's here!!!! Can't you see Him in yourself and others? Are you the same today you were before you accepted Him? Are you the same even last week or last year? Who's changing you? It certainly isn't you! From where is the change coming? From within! Why? Because, He is in there changing you. Then why stand you gazing UP?

YOU ARE HIS TEMPLE

1 Cor. 3:16-17 Know ye not that ye are the temple of God, and that the Spirit of God dwelleth in you? If any man defile the temple of God, him shall God destroy; for the temple of God is holy, which temple ye are. If God already has a temple, why would He need one off in the blue yonder or to return and set up another one?

1 Cor. 6:15, 19-20 Know ye not that your BODIES are the members of Christ? shall I then take the members of Christ, and make them the members of a harlot? God forbid. --- What! know ye not that your body is the temple of the Holy Ghost which is in you, which ye have of God, and ye are not your own? For ye are bought with a price: therefore glorify God in your body, and in your spirit, which are God's.

2 Cor. 13:5 Examine yourselves, whether ye be in the faith; prove your own selves, how that Jesus Christ is IN you, except ye be reprobates?

There are many, many more scriptures that bear out that we

are the temple of God. A King's temple or palace sets in the midst of the King's kingdom. If He is in us, where would that put His kingdom?

JESUS COMING IN US

2 Cor. 6:16 And what agreement hath the temple of God with idols? for ye are the temple of the living God; as God hath said, I will dwell <u>in</u> them, and walk <u>in</u> them; and I will be their God, and they shall be my people.

Where is He dwelling? In us. Where is He walking? In us. This is why we need to be very careful not to allow idols in this temple (things that become an idol to us) or to defile it (abuse our body). How can He bring us LIFE if we are constantly defiling our bodies and allowing death to enter? We are working against Him.

Paul says in *Gal. 1:15-16* that he was called in his mother's womb. Why? Because God wanted to reveal His Son in Paul. This shows us where the Son will be revealed, in us. *Gal. 2:20* Paul says that he is crucified with Christ. When we accept Him as our Savior, we, too, are crucified with Him. Paul says, 'Nevertheless I live; yet not I, but Christ liveth *IN* me. We are dead, but alive, because He is doing the living out of us (if we will let Him).

Gal. 4:19 says Christ is being **FORMED IN US.** This is why we don't see Him as full grown in us. As a natural fetus goes through stages and is formed in us, so is He. We don't carry a natural baby inside us forever, do we? Eventually, the Spirit of Christ that is being formed in us will be born outward for all to see.

2 Thes. 1:10 When he shall come to be glorified in his saints, and to be admired in all them that believe (because our testimony among you was believed) in that day.

He is going to be glorified and to be admired IN all His saints. Are you one of His saints? In *Heb. 3:6,* we find out that we are the house of Christ, and, in *Heb. 8:2* we see that we are the true tabernacle and Christ is the minister in it. *Heb. 9:11* talks about Christ becoming a high priest over a greater and more perfect tabernacle than the natural one in the feast sacrifices. We are that greater and more perfect tabernacle not made with hands and Christ is the high priest ministering out of the Holy of Holies, our spirit.

1 Peter 2:5 Ye also, as lively stones, are built up a spiritual house, a holy priesthood, to offer up spiritual sacrifices, acceptable to God by Jesus Christ.

Did you notice the word 'spiritual'? We each are those stones that together will build that spiritual house. If it is to be a spiritual house; then, we need to quit looking for a natural one.

Luke 17:20-21 And when he was demanded of the Pharisees, when the kingdom of God should come, he answered them and said, The kingdom of God cometh not with observation: Neither shall they say, Lo here! or, lo there! For, behold, the kingdom of God is within you.

My, my. How much plainer does Jesus have to say it? The kingdom of God is not coming with signs in the literal clouds to be observed; but, behold -- it is WITHIN you. He is wherever His kingdom is.

Matt. 23:39 For I say unto you, Ye shall not see me henceforth, till ye shall say, Blessed is he that cometh in the name of the Lord.

Who comes in the name or nature of the Lord? I do. You do. You will not see Him until you can see Him in yourself and others. Why have we not been able to see Him in our brethren? We can't get past each others faults. We do not look through the eyes of the Spirit.

COMING IN CLOUDS

Remember symbolism? How did God lead the children of Israel in the wilderness? By a cloud during the day and a pillar of fire at night. There was light provided both day and night. Spiritually, God has provided light or knowledge of Him even during the darkest time of each thousand year days. How did He appear in the tabernacle? He appeared in a 'cloud' at the door of the tabernacle. Images, images, images. When we read these scriptures, automatically, we see images of natural clouds out here. Okay. Let's look at them. If the natural sun represents the spiritual son, Jesus; and, the natural sun shines through the natural clouds, what would Jesus be shining through? Spiritual clouds. Let's find out what the spiritual clouds are.

2 Peter 2:17 These are wells without water, clouds that are carried with a tempest; to whom the mist of darkness is reserved for ever.

If you will read the first of the chapter, you will discover that the clouds are referring to men that have gone astray from the teachings of Christ and have become false prophets. They are wells without water or, in other words, they haven't the spirit of Christ. They are blown here and yon by the storms of life.

58

Jude 1:12 These are spots in your feasts of charity, when they feast with you, feeding themselves without fear: clouds they are without water, carried about of winds; trees whose fruit withereth, without fruit, twice dead, plucked up by the roots;

Jude is referring to certain men that had infiltrated the church with other teachings. He says they are without the spirit and can be carried away by any doctrine, because they do not have a foundation or anchor in Christ. He is warning the people about them. He refers to them as trees that cannot produce fruit.

Heb. 12:1 tells us that we are compassed about by a great cloud of witnesses. Who are these clouds of witnesses? Those that have crossed into the realm of the invisible that were in Christ. They are cheering us on to finish the race set before us. When we win, they become winners. *Heb. 11:40* says that they without us should not be made perfect (WHOLE OR COMPLETE) because God has provided a better thing for us to obtain -- *LIFE*.

I hope I have said and shown enough proof of the 'true' coming of Christ in His body that you are able to see it is a spiritual catching up in Him. While some will still be looking up, He will come in as a thief through the back door and catch them unawares. If you cannot spiritually 'see', then, the mystery is still hidden to you. Ask the Holy Spirit to give you ***ears to hear*** and ***eyes to see*** the mystery.

LET'S REVIEW:

1. Who was the original source of the Rapture doctrine?

2. Who brought it to the United States?

3. From whose footnotes did the doctrine spring?

4. What does the word 'caught up' mean?

5. How did Jesus go away in *Acts 1*?

6. When did He return?

7. How did He return?

8. *John* says that Jesus and the Holy Ghost are the Spirit of what?
9. Who was the comforter to come?

10. Where is Jesus and the Father making their abode?

11. Why did Jesus have to go away?

12. What type of word is 'coming'?

13. What is a kingdom?

14. What did Jesus pray about his charge (people John 17:15)?

15. What does it take to enter the Kingdom of God?

16. What works patience?

17. According to *Col. 1:13,* from what has Jesus delivered us?

18. Where did He take us?

19. What represents our full salvation?

20. When will we appear and how?

21. Who witnessed the Son of man coming in His kingdom?

22. What does *Romans* tell us that the kingdom is?

23. Where is it found?

24. Where does the Holy Ghost dwell?

25. Where does that place the Kingdom of God?

26. Righteousness, joy and peace describes what?

27. Of what does *1 Cor. 4:20* say the Kingdom of God consists?

28. For what are we being fitly framed together?

29. You are God's what and what dwells in you?

30. Our bodies are what (1 *Cor. 6:15*)?

31. Where are we to glorify God?

32. Where is God going to dwell and walk?

33. Where will the Son be revealed?

34. What does *Gal. 4:19* tell you about Christ?

35. If we want to see Him, where must we look?

36. Who is the greater and more perfect tabernacle not made with hands?

37. We are called lively stones to build up what?

38. In *Luke,* when did Jesus say the Kingdom would come and where?

39. How did God lead the children of Israel in the wilderness?

40. What are clouds symbolizing?

41. Who are the great cloud of witnesses?

42. What are we to obtain?

NOTES:

† Chapter 5 †

Born Again Man

Hopefully, in the last chapter, I was able to present clearly enough for you to 'see' that the true rapture will take place spiritually in you; and, the true *'coming'* of Jesus Christ has happened, is happening, and will continue to happen until He is fully grown or mature in us. When we are speaking and doing as we hear Him speak and do, we have been swallowed up or fully seized by the spirit of Christ and are fully manifesting His nature in the earth.

During this process of growth, we learn and then do. One thing we must try to understand is what man is, what he is becoming; and, in order to start the journey, he must be born again.

First, let's establish all that man is.

Gen. 1:26-27 And God said, Let us make man in our image, after our likeness: and let them have dominion over the fish of the sea, and over the fowl of the air, and over the cattle, and over all the earth, and over every creeping thing that creepeth upon the earth. So God **created** *man in his own image, in the image of God created he him; male and female created he him.*

Gen. 5:2 Male and female created he them; and blessed them, and called their name Adam, in the day when they were created.

Man is male and female called 'Adam' or Red Man. The man (kind) we see created is the Adamic race. 'Image' means shade, illusion, resemblance; a representative figure. It wasn't the body of man that was created in His image, but his spirit. Mankind was a shade, an illusion or representative figure of God in the earthy realm. We see that God gave mankind dominion or rulership over all things in this realm. The word 'God' used in this verse is plural meaning magistrates with God. *Psa. 82;6; Isa. 41:23; and, John 10:34* all say 'ye are gods.' Why are we gods (with a little g)? Because we are children of the most High God. Kings have princes and princesses don't they? These offsprings are given the authority of the father when they mature, are they not? They grow up to sit on the throne.

If *Gen. 1* is a spiritual picture of the plan and purpose of God through the ages and His magistrates (us) are to carry out this plan, then the dominion given to man is over these things spiritually. Even naturally, God gave us dominion or an intelligence over these natural subjects. They represent spiritual things that are produced in you that you must subdue or prevail against. Example: fear, hate, lust, jealousy, backbiting, adultery, fornication, witchcraft (rebellion), envyings, and the list goes on and on. This is what the works of the flesh will produce if you do not exercise dominion over or subdue the flesh by the spirit. We see man first as a spirit or a representative figure of God in the earth.

Second, man is a living soul or he is given emotions and given the ability to make choices. He can now think and reason.

*Gen. 2:7 And the Lord God **formed** man of the dust of the ground, and breathed in his nostrils the breath of life; and man became a living soul.*

1 Cor. 15:45 And so it is written, The first man Adam was made a living soul; the last Adam was made a quickening (life giving) spirit.

In the first day, we see man living out of the soul or his own intellect and emotions. Man's soul is no longer under the rulership or dominion of the spirit. Man begins to react to his environment instead of acting out of his spirit. Jesus never reacted to anything that happened to or around Him. He always acted according to what the scriptures said or what He heard His father say. He did not allow His emotions or intellect to rule Him. Thus, He becomes the last man Adam; no longer ruled by soul, but He becomes a quickening or life giving spirit. Everyone coming after Him, believing in Him, becomes a new creature in Him. We are His offspring, the new creation man. *Acts 8:33* asks 'who will declare his generation for his life is taken from the earth?' Jesus' offspring that were to carry on His name were to be spiritual not natural. We are that generation to declare His name or nature in the earth.

Third, man has a body.

Gen. 3:21 Unto Adam also and to his wife did the Lord God make coats of skins, and clothed them.

Remember, 'Adam' includes male and female and his wife represents his soul. The spirit and soul are housed in skins or the body. This is why, through the making of the tabernacle, ram's skins were used to signify our earthy house and carnal nature. Thus far we see mankind is spirit with a soulish nature housed in a body.

Fourth, man is the salt of the earth.

Matt. 5:13 Ye are the salt of the earth: but if the salt have lost his savour, wherewith shall it be salted? it is thenceforth good for nothing, but to be cast out, and to be trodden under foot of men.

Salt means: preserve; prudence or foresight to avoid error or danger.

Lose savour means: to become dull, stupid, heedless, passive action.

We are salt or we were given the ability to avoid error or danger, through Christ. If we lose that ability, we become dull, stupid, passive action.

Fifth, we are the righteousness of God.

2 Cor. 5:21 For he hath made him to be sin for us, who knew no sin; that we might be made the righteousness of God in him.

Righteousness means: right justice; the principle, a decision, or its execution. Plain and simple, we are to make the right decision or judgment call according to the spirit and carry it out. Notice it says that we might be 'made' His righteousness, or in other words, to come into being in the ability to make the right decisions and then carry them out. It is obvious, as our lives have proven it, that in ourselves, we cannot make the right decisions 100% of the time.

How can we? How do we become His righteousness in the earth?

Rom. 3:21-22 But now the righteousness of God without the law is manifested, being witnessed by the law and the prophets; even the righteousness of God which is by faith of Jesus Christ unto all and upon all them that believe: for there is no difference.

It isn't by keeping 'man made' religious laws that will manifest His righteousness.

Rom. 3:23-27 For all have sinned, and come short of the glory of God; Being justified freely by his grace through the redemption that is in Christ Jesus: Whom God hath set forth to be a propitiation through faith in his blood, to declare his righteousness for the remission of sins that are past, through the forbearance of God; to declare, I say, at this time his righteousness: that he might be just, and the justifier of him which believeth in Jesus. Where is boasting then? It is excluded. By what law? of works? Nay: but by the law of faith.

By the law of faith, we are freely given, through Christ's redemption, the ability to make right decisions and to execute them. What's the catch? Why do we continue to make wrong decisions?

Rom. 3:28-31 Therefore we conclude that a man is justified by faith without the deeds of the law. Is he the God of the Jews only? Is he not also of the Gentiles? Yes, of the Gentiles also: Seeing it is one God, which shall justify the circumcision by faith, and uncircumcision through faith. Do we then make void the law through faith? God forbid: yea, we establish the law.

We don't do away with the law, we establish it or fulfill it as Christ said He did in *Matt. 5:17-18*. How do we fulfill the law?

Rom. 13:8 Owe no man any thing, but to love one another: for he that loveth another hath fulfilled the law.

We must love one another; no ifs, ands, or buts. Point blank, to fulfill the law, we have to love one another as Christ has loved us.

Rom. 10:3 For they being ignorant of God's righteousness, and going about to establish their own righteousness, have not submitted themselves unto the righteousness of God.

The key word here is 'submitted.' We have to submit ourselves to His righteousness or the way He makes decisions and executes them through Christ. Don't just invite Christ to come in and sit down on your throne. Give Him the scepter and let Him be the ruler of your house. Through Him, you will make the right decisions and will have the ability to carry them out. What is man? He is a spirit with a soul, housed in a body. By avoiding error and becoming and executing the righteousness of God on earth, he becomes the salt or preservative of the earth.

To realize and produce this, we must be born again. Over the years, one would publicly announce that he/she wanted Christ to come into their heart. Some changed, some didn't. Why? Many think they have salvation; but, let's measure our present idea of 'salvation' by the word. If you find any part in yourself lacking, strengthen it by truly committing your **ALL;** body, soul, and spirit.

Matt. 7:15 Beware of false prophets, which come to you in sheep's clothing, but inwardly they are ravening wolves.

I was always taught the above scripture referred to someone who was preaching a false word in the name of the Lord. Let me give you another example. What are sheep, spiritually speaking? They are God's saints. What does wearing sheep's clothing mean? It means if we are one of His sheep, we are clothed in Him. Then, who would be the false prophets? They are the ones who are outwardly declaring that they are His sheep, but, inwardly they are not. We need to take stock of our spirit and see if we are truly sheep or ravenous wolves. What is your spirit producing? *Gal. 5:17-23* gives us a list of the fruits that our spirit will be producing if we walk after flesh or if we walk after the spirit. Use this to measure whether you are walking after the spirit or walking after the flesh.

John 3:3 Jesus answered and said unto him, verily, verily, I say unto thee, except a man be born again, he cannot see the kingdom of God.

You must know what 'born again' means before you can experience it; and, unless you experience it, you cannot see the Kingdom of God. *Born* means: to procreate; figurative to regenerate: bear, beget, be born, bring forth, conceive, be delivered of, gender, make, spring. Look at the first part of the word 'Generation': Gene. You become a part of His seedline or of His genes, that promised generation. Through the hearing of the word and the spirit moving on it, a seed is planted in you, as was in Mary. As you ponder it, as she did, and the spirit moves on it, you conceive and begin to bring forth. Mary produced Jesus; the word was made flesh. We will produce a word in the flesh, spiritually speaking. That word will be produced in us. We will begin to produce the fruits of righteousness.

First, you are born by the word; and then, you give birth by the word. My mother gave birth to me then I turned and gave birth to my child. My spiritual mother gave birth to me by planting the word in me. I conceived that word and have turned and given birth by teaching this word to others who received it. Not everyone who hears the word will conceive. If you are not seeing an outward change in your life, then, either you truly haven't experienced a rebirth or you have a barren womb. Either way, you need to surrender before God and take this first step so that you can 'see' the Kingdom of God.

See means: to know, to perceive, to understand. You truly cannot see your full inheritance if you don't 'see' the Kingdom of God. There are steps to take to receive your *FULL* inheritance and they have to be taken in order, leaving none out. The first step begins with the rebirth and progressing forward.

Matt. 18:3 And said, Verily I say unto you, except ye be converted, and become as little children, ye shall not enter into the kingdom of heaven.

This does not mean that you will physically become as a little child. **Converted** means to turn around or reverse directions. Why little children? God wants you to totally depend and trust in Him without doubt, committing your all and holding nothing back for yourself. This is the way children are. They totally trust and depend on their parents to take care of them.

After you have 'seen' or understood the kingdom, you must enter it and begin to live as a citizen of the kingdom.

John 3:7-8 Marvel not that I said unto thee, Ye must be born again. The wind bloweth where it listeth, and thou hearest the sound thereof, but canst not tell whence it cometh, and whither it goeth. so is every one that is born of the Spirit.

It is not for us to question. It is done by faith.

John 20:31 But these are written, that ye might believe that Jesus is the Christ, the Son of God; and that believing ye might have life through his name.

This does not just mean life here after. *Col. 1:13* says the minute you are reborn, Jesus translates you into His Kingdom. It will be up to you whether you continue to wear your garment of skins or not, physically live or die.

John 5:24 Verily, verily, I say unto you, He that heareth my word, and believeth on him that sent me, hath everlasting life, and shall not come into condemnation; but is passed from death unto life.

John 3:15 That whosoever believeth in him should not perish, but have eternal life.

This word 'believeth' doesn't mean just giving lip service by saying you are a Christian. It means having complete faith in who Jesus was and is, and that no matter what, He is in full control. No doubt, no fear. He desires that no man perish or physically die, but live and have life everlasting.

John 3:16-18 For God so loved the world, that he gave his only begotten Son, that whosoever believeth in him should not perish, but have everlasting (perpetual) life. For God sent not his Son into the world to condemn the world; but that the world through him might be saved. He that believeth on him is not condemned: but he that believeth not it condemned already, because he hath not believed in the name of the only begotten Son of God.

Jesus came to condemn the orderly arrangement of that day. He didn't come to condemn man because man was already condemned. Man was living in sin which was producing death. Jesus came to bring man out of condemnation and death. Being truly born again translates us out of the state of condemnation and into His Kingdom. Right then, at that translation, perpetual or eternal life begins; not after you die. Sin and death can't touch you as long as you stay in and operate out of the heavenlies or His Kingdom. Just as a natural Kingdom has walls around the city to protect the inhabitants, so is it with the Kingdom of God. As long as you stay within the city, you are protected by the walls or boundaries set by God. It only takes being outside the walls one time for the enemy to get you, take you hostage or kill you then and there.

If you want to know what will bring life or death and what sin or missing the mark is, read: *Rom. 6:12-16, 22-23; Rom. 8:13; Gal. 5; Eph. 5.*

John 11:25-26 Jesus said unto her, I am the resurrection (standing up again), and the life: he that believeth in me, though he were dead, yet shall he live: And whosoever liveth and believeth in me shall never die. Believest thou this?

I ask you today, believest thou this? Do you believe that you can physically live and not die? I'm not talking about living in the current condition you are in now; but, in a changed state. The only sacrifice you truly make when you totally surrender to God is sacrificing death for life. In the next few chapters, I hope to show you what was lost in Adam and restored through Christ, LIFE. Please, don't leave me now. I will explain how LIFE was lost, how it was restored, and eternal LIFE.

LET'S REVIEW:

1. To whom was God referring when he called them Adam?

2. Who is to carry out the plan and purpose of God? They are known as?

3. What does the word 'image' mean?

4. Spiritually, over what are we to have dominion?

5. What is man first?

6. What is he second?

7. What is man's soul?

8. What does Adam's wife represent?

9. In what are the spirit and soul housed?

10. What does 'salt' mean?

11. If you lose your savour, you become what?

12. What does 'righteousness' mean?

13. Not only are we to make the right decisions in God, but we are to what?

14. How do we become His righteousness?

15. What law gives you the ability to make right decisions and then execute them?

16. What are we to do with the Mosaic law?

17. What does *Rom. 13:8* tell us to do?

18. What will the results be?

19. What do we have to do unto the righteousness of God?

20. What are sheep, spiritually speaking?

21. What is a sheep's clothing?

22. What is the false prophet?

23. What will the ravenous wolves produce?

24. What will true sheep produce?

25. What does a man have to do to see the Kingdom of God?

26. What word can be found in 'generation'?

27. Who did not have a generation to declare him?

28. How do you become a part of his seedline?

29. By what are you birthed?

30. What do you birth?

31. If you are not giving birth, what is wrong?

32. What does the word 'see' mean?

33. What must you be and then become to enter into the Kingdom?

34. What happens to you the minute you are reborn?

35. What does condemnation bring?

36. What did Jesus come to do?

37. Where are we if we don't believe on Him?

38. What translates you out of condemnation?

39. What are you sacrificing when you become reborn?

NOTES:

† Chapter 6 †

Why Did Jesus Die?

If Jesus were to set up a literal kingdom, there would not have been a need for His death. This was not His role in the plan and purpose of God. Before disobedience, man lived and did not die. Because of the choice that Adam made, a curse of death was placed on mankind. There is always an antidote for every poison. God gave the woman a promise that she would bring forth in great sorrow; but, her seed would bruise the head of the serpent.

Gen. 3:2-3 And the woman said unto the serpent, We may eat of the fruit of the trees of the garden: But of the fruit of the tree which is in the midst of the garden, God hath said, Ye shall not eat of it, neither shall ye touch it, lest ye die.

Gen. 3:21 Unto Adam also and to his wife did the Lord God make coats of skins, and clothed them.

Man has taught, by assumption, that God killed an animal and clothed Adam. Why not assume that the skins that make up your body could be the skins with which He clothed them? It is a proven fact that your body will adapt to its environment. The Adamic race was so in tune with the voice of God that they lived in a higher state spiritually, mentally, and physically. When they began to live out of the soul or by intellect and emotions, it caused their body to adapt accordingly. When they were cast out of the garden or an intimate place with God, they lost LIFE.

Gen. 3:22 And the Lord God said, Behold, the man is become as one of us, to know good and evil: and now, lest he put forth his hand, and take also of the tree of life, and eat, and LIVE FOREVER.

Adam had being eating from the Tree of Life, God. If he continued to eat of it and live forever, he would live out of the soul and not out of the spirit of God. This was part of the plan of God. The imperfect Adam was only a figure of Him to come, the perfect man Jesus.

Jesus had to walk every step man had walked and He had to defeat everything that had defeated man, including death. He had to fulfill the scriptures and reverse the curse. He did not have to die; but, that was God's plan.

Matt. 26:53-54 Thinkest thou that I cannot now pray to my Father, and he shall presently give me more than twelve legions of angels? But how then shall the scriptures be fulfilled, that thus it must be?

John 19:11 Jesus answered, Thou couldest have no power at all against me, except it were given thee from above: therefore he that delivered me unto thee hath the greater sin.

John 19:28-30 After this, Jesus knowing that all things were now accomplished, that the scripture might be Fulfilled, saith, I thirst. Now there was set a vessel full of vinegar: and they filled a spunge with vinegar, and put it upon hyssop, and put it to his mouth. When Jesus therefore had received the vinegar, he said, It is finished: and he bowed his head, and gave up the ghost.

Jesus gave up His spirit. It was not taken from Him. He had accomplished what He had come to do: fulfill the scriptures and show us the way back to the Tree of Life.

1 Cor. 15:21-22 For since by man came death, by man came also the resurrection of the dead. For as in Adam all die, even so in Christ shall all be made alive.

1 Cor. 15:26 The last enemy that shall be destroyed is death.

Why would death need to be destroyed unless we were to live and not die? Spiritual death was destroyed already. Jesus had to lay down His natural body, go into the realm of the dead, defeat death on that side and rescue those that were held captive there, return to this realm and take up His body for those to see that He had defeated death on this side.

Psa. 68:18 Thou hast ascended on high, thou hast led captivity captive (those in death): thou hast received gifts for men; yea, for the rebellious also, that the Lord God might dwell among them.

Jesus released those in death and darkness and brought them into light and life. He did this even for the rebellious, because God desires to dwell with men again.

Eph. 4:8 Wherefore he saith, When he ascended up on high, he led captivity captive, and gave gifts unto men.

Matt. 27:52-53 And the graves were opened; and many bodies of the saints which slept arose, And came out of the graves after his resurrection, and went into the holy city, and appeared unto many.

In a later chapter, I will discuss what the graves were. People on this side were able to see those that had crossed into the invisible realm. To me, this shows a foreshadowing of what is to be. Do not get an image in your mind of the ghost movies we see of the walking dead. They are walking in light.

John 10:10 The thief cometh not, but for to steal, and to kill, and to destroy: I am come that they might have life, and that they might have it more abundantly.

Jesus said He came to bring life. Where did He come? To this earthy realm. Then, where are we to have life? Here. Not temporary life, but, life abundantly; perpetual life.

John 10:15-16 As the Father knoweth me, even so know I the Father: and I lay down my life for the sheep. And other sheep I have, which are not of this fold: them also I must bring, and they shall hear my voice; and there shall be one fold, and one shepherd.

He laid down His life for all but, who are the other sheep? Those on the other side. He must bring all together, making one fold. He had a job to do on both sides of the 'river.'

John 10:17-18 Therefore doth my Father love me, because I lay down my life, that I might take it again. No man taketh it from me, but I lay it down of myself. I have power to lay it down, and I have power to take it again. This commandment have I received of my Father.

Do you think He delighted in what He knew He had to do to finish this job? You may say, 'Yes because He WAS JESUS!' He was no different than you and me in the flesh. He allowed Himself to be totally ruled by the Spirit of the Father God. He believed, without a shadow of a doubt, everything that His Father told Him. This is where we differ from Jesus. We allow doubt to enter in instead of totally trusting and doing the will of the Father.

Luke 22:41-44 And he was withdrawn from them about a stone's cast, and kneeled down, and prayed, Saying, Father, if thou be willing, remove this cup from me: nevertheless not my will, but thine, be done. And there appeared an angel unto him from heaven, strengthening him. And being in an agony he prayed more earnestly: and his sweat was as it were great drops of blood falling down to the ground.

It didn't matter what Jesus wanted. He proved it when He prayed 'if thou be willing, remove this cup.' He only wanted it removed if it was in the plan and purpose of God. He looked beyond Himself and what He wanted and looked into the eons of time of what would be accomplished through His crucifixion. He believed God when He was told He had all power, even to lay down and pick up His life again. How did He use this power? Did He use it as His Father would or did He use it to benefit Himself? How would we use this power? We really need to consider this, because, only the mature Sons of God will be given this power.

After Jesus completed His job on the other side, He came and took up His body.

John 20:14-16 And when she had thus said, she turned herself back, and saw Jesus standing, and knew not that it was Jesus. Jesus saith unto her, Woman, why weepest thou? whom seekest thou? She supposing him to be the gardener, saith unto him, Sir, if thou have borne him hence, tell me where thou hast laid him, and I will take him away. Jesus saith unto her, Mary. She turned herself, and saith unto him, Rabboni; which is to say, Master.

Mary didn't know Jesus by sight because of His transfiguration; but, she recognized His voice only after He called her by name. Many of us only know the person Jesus; and, when He wants to take us to another level in Him, we don't recognize Him because He isn't presenting Himself the way we knew Him. Only until He calls us by our name or nature, do we realize that it is Him.

Mark 16:12 After that he appeared in another form unto two of them, as they walked, and went into the country.

Luke 24:15-17 And it came to pass, that, while they communed together and reasoned, Jesus himself drew near, and went with them. But their eyes were holden that they should not know him. And he said unto them, What manner of communications are these that ye have one to another, as ye walk, and are said?

Holden means to seize or retain. They were not seeing or understanding by their spiritual eyes.

Luke 24:30-31 And it came to pass, as he sat at meat with them, he took bread, and blessed it, and brake it, and gave to them. And their eyes were opened, and they knew him; and he vanished out of their sight.

Opened means to open thoroughly or to expound. When they recognized Him spiritually, they no longer beheld Him with physical eyes. They 'saw' Him differently.

Acts 1:3 To whom also he shewed himself alive after his passion by many infallible proofs, being seen of them forty days, and speaking of the things pertaining to the kingdom of God:

Luke 24:36-48 And as they thus spake, Jesus himself stood in the midst of them, and saith unto them, Peace be unto you. But they were terrified and affrighted, and supposed that they had seen a spirit. And he said unto them, Why are ye troubled? and why do thoughts arise in your hearts? Behold my hands and my feet, that it is I myself: handle me, and see; for a spirit hath not flesh and bones, as ye see me have. And when he had thus spoken, he shewed them his hands and his feet. And while they yet believed not for joy, and wondered, he said unto them, Have ye here any meat? And they gave him a piece of a broiled fish, and of an honeycomb. And he took it, and did eat before them. And he said unto them, These are the words which I spake unto you, while I was yet with you, that all things must be fulfilled, which were written in the law of Moses, and in the prophets, and in the psalms, concerning me. Then opened he their understanding, that they might understand the scriptures, And said unto them, Thus it is written, and thus it behooved Christ to suffer, and to rise from the dead the third day: And that repentance and remission of sins should be preached in his name among all nations, beginning at Jerusalem. And ye are witnesses of these things.

When Christ wants to reveal more of Himself to us, we reject Him or can't believe it's Him because it does not live with the religious traditions of our forefathers. We are afraid and say it is heresy. It didn't matter what Jesus did then or what He does today to prove it is Him, there still were and are today doubters.

John 20:24-31 But Thomas, one of the twelve, called Diadems, was not with them when Jesus came. The other disciples therefore said unto him, We have seen the Lord. But he said unto them, Except I shall see in his hands the print of the nails, and put my finger into the print of the nails, and thrust my hand into his side, I will not believe. And after eight days again his disciples were within, and Thomas with them: then came Jesus, the doors being shut, and stood in the midst, and said, Peace be unto you. Then saith he to Thomas, reach hither thy finger, and behold my hands; and reach hither thy hand, and thrust it into my side: and be not faithless, but believing. And Thomas answered and said unto him, My Lord and my God. Jesus saith unto him, Thomas, because thou hast seen me, thou hast believed: blessed are they that have not seen, and yet have believed. And many other signs truly did Jesus in the presence of his disciples, which are not written in this book: But these are written, that ye might believe that Jesus is the Christ, the Son of God; and that believing ye might have LIFE through his name.

Thomas had to have a physical sign to believe. He had to go by feeling. Does this sound familiar? Have you ever said, "But, I can't feel the presence of God?" We walk by what the Word says, not according to a feeling. If we always measure the presence of God by a feeling, we will miss Him many, many times.

Jesus Christ defeated death in Himself and restored the Way back to Life. We are to follow after Him. He was the firstborn among many brethren *(Rom. 8:29)*. *Heb. 9:15* says Jesus was the mediator of the new testament, that they which were called might receive the inheritance of eternal life. A will is only opened and probated at the death of the testator. The testament is of no strength as long as the testator lives.

To receive and spend the inheritance, the heir must be alive. If you physically die, you lose your full inheritance. Jesus became that quickening or life giving spirit. Where does He dwell? In us, right? Then, where would that life quickening spirit be? In us. The scriptures say that if you walk after the Spirit, your reward will be life; but, if you walk after the lust of the flesh, your reward will be sin unto death.

In the next chapter I hope to show you how LIFE was restored and discuss what eternal LIFE is.

LET'S REVIEW:

1. What brought the curse of death upon man?

2. What would be the result of eating of the knowledge?

3. With what did God clothe Adam and his wife?

4. What did his wife represent?

5. What would have been the result if Adam continued to partake of the Tree of Life?

6. What did Jesus have to defeat?

7. Why could they not take Jesus' life?

8. Why did He not have His Father call twelve legions of angels?

9. What did Jesus give up after drinking the vinegar?

10. How did death enter into the world?

11. Through whom was life restored?

12. What is the last enemy to be destroyed?

13. Where did Jesus go after His crucifixion?

14. Who did Jesus Christ lead captive after His crucifixion?

15. After Jesus' resurrection, who appeared to many and was seen walking in the holy city for many days?

16. Jesus said He came to this world that we might have what?

17. Who is He bringing into one fold?

18. What let's you know Jesus was willing but dreading His fate?

19. Who did Mary think Jesus was at first?

20. When did she realize who He was?

21. How did He appear to the two walking on the road?

22. In *Luke,* why were the men unable to realize who was with them?

23. When did they realize who He was? What were they doing at the time?

24. How long did He stay with them before His ascension?

25. When He stood in the midst of His disciples, what did they think He was?

26. How did He try to convince them who He was?

27. What did He finally do so they could understand who He was?

28. Who had to have physical evidence?

29. Who was more blessed than Thomas and why?

30. Jesus is the mediator of what?

31. What was the promise of the new testament?

32. What must a testator be for the will to be opened?

33. Did Jesus follow this pattern?

34. Jesus was the firstborn among whom?

35. What kind of spirit did Jesus become?

36. What did mankind lose in Adam?

37. What was restored through Jesus Christ?

38. What does 'perpetual' mean?

NOTES:

† *Chapter 7* †

Restored Life Eternal

With our western carnal thinking, we rationalize that it is impossible to live in this earth forever, especially since all we've known is death, so the scriptures MUST be referring to life AFTER death. Allow your spiritual ears and eyes to be opened and just ponder this.

Psa. 23:3 He restoreth my soul: he leadeth me in the paths of righteousness for his name's sake.

Restore means: return back or return or reverse. What is He restoring? Our soul. When was it lost? When Adam made the wrong choice in the garden or in his body. The separation of spirit and soul brought death because the soul was no longer under the dominion and rulership of the spirit. When the soul comes in line with the spirit of God in us and submits to it, we will see life reigning once again.

Jer. 30:17 For I will restore health unto thee, and I will heal thee of thy wounds, saith the Lord; because they called thee an Outcast, saying, This is Zion, whom no man seeketh after.

What is He restoring? Our health is being restored and our wounds healed.

Joel 2:25 And I will restore to you the years that the locust hath eaten, the cankerworm, and the caterpillar, and the palmerworm, my great army which I sent among you.

The word **Locust** means: Increase. **Cankerworm** means: To lick up, a devourer, the young locust. **Caterpillar** means: The ravager, to eat off, consume such as a locust. **Palmerworm** means: To devour, a kind of locust.

God said this was His great army that He had sent among us. These all represent things in our lives that has robbed us of life. Through Jesus Christ, God made a way back to the garden, and said what we lost would be restored.

Matt. 12:13 Then saith he to the man, Stretch forth thine hand. And he stretched it forth; and it was restored whole, like as the other.

Mark 8:25 After that he put his hands again upon his eyes, and made him look up: and he was restored, and saw every man clearly.

In each of these scriptures, we see that something is being restored and these people were very much alive.

John 3:15 That whosoever believeth in him should not perish, but have eternal life.

Perish means: to destroy fully, DIE, lose, mar. *Eternal* means: a Messianic period, perpetual, course. *Perpetual* means: constant without a break; ongoing. *Life* means: to live, period.

1 John 5:11 And this is the record (evidence given), that God hath given to us eternal life, and this life is in his Son.

What is this record? That God has given us life through Jesus Christ. The scripture didn't say life after you die. How do we get it? We have to believe and *believe* is the big catch. We say we believe only if it is logical to us.

We need to take a closer look and realize that this is for now and not sometime in the future. We have been given a gift and we are not accepting it. We have been given the gift to live perpetually, without interruption by death; but, we are not listening nor are we truly taking it to heart. If we were, our lives would not be going on 'as usual.'

John 6:54 Whoso eateth my flesh (word), and drinketh my blood (spirit, life), hath eternal life; and I will raise him up at the last day.

We take this to mean that we will be resurrected after death. Jesus is saying if you will perpetually consume my word and wash yourself in the spirit, I will awaken or lift you up out of death to stand in the last day or dispensation, which is the dispensation of His Kingdom. We are passing from the dispensation of Grace into the dispensation of Kingdom, where He will rule and reign out of His body, the saints.

John 10:28 And I give unto them eternal life; and they shall never perish, neither shall any man pluck them out of my hand.

Even literally reading the scripture tells you that you will not die; but, it doesn't fit our logic, thus it must mean our spirit will never die. A spirit can't die. It can't be referring to your spirit.

Rom. 2:7 To them who by patient continuance in well doing seek for glory and honour and immortality, eternal life.

Through patient continuance, we are to SEEK for glory and honour and IMMORTALITY. ***Immortality*** means not capable of dying, un-decaying, an unending existence. Your spirit man is already immortal and it can't decay; so, this is not referring to your spirit man. What makes you decay? Sin or missing the mark that Christ has set before us.

Rom. 5:21 That as sin hath reigned unto death, even so might grace reign through righteousness unto eternal life by Jesus Christ our Lord.

Rom. 6:23 For the wages of sin is death; but the gift of God is eternal life through Jesus Christ our Lord.

Does this say death after death or spiritual death? No.

1 John 5:20 And we know that the Son of God is come, and hath given us an understanding, that we may know him that is true, and we are in him that is true, even in his Son Jesus Christ. This is the true God, and eternal life.

Jesus showed us how to walk upright before God. He gave us the understanding of His Word by the Holy Spirit; but, what are we doing with it? He has told us the plan and purpose of God; but yet, we choose to live in vanity (*Eccl*). We would rather believe a fairy tale and die than the truth and live. If we believed the truth, we would have to do something about it. We would have to totally change our way of thinking, which would change our way of living. There are too many things we like about the world to let it go.

1 Tim. 6:19 Laying hold in store for themselves a good foundation against the time to come, that they may lay hold on (seize) eternal life.

Titus 1:2 In hope of eternal life, which God, that cannot lie, promised before the world began;

When did God promise it? This tells me that He intended for us to live and not die.

1 John 2:25 And this is the promise that he hath promised us, even eternal life.

This is a promise given to us and God cannot lie. He keeps His promises.

1 John 1:2 (For the life (Jesus) was manifested, and we have seen it, and bear witness, and shew unto you that eternal life, which was with the Father, and was manifested unto us;)

We do not have an excuse for not knowing how to have life because this verse clearly says life was manifested before us and we have witness of it. It is no longer something unseen, but, is made visible for us. Jesus Christ is eternal life. He walked an uninterrupted life with God. He wasn't on today and off tomorrow. He didn't give God excuses like: 'I just don't have time.' 'I've got to do this first.' 'If I didn't have to be around these kind of people, I could live a righteous life.'

What would God have done had Jesus lived His life according

to His excuses? Yet, we think it's okay for us to live our life like that. Jesus was able to do what He did because He lived an uninterrupted life in God. According to scripture, the wages of sin are death. Jesus did not sin, therefore, He would have lived on in God, uninterrupted by death. Death did not take Him. Scripture says Jesus 'gave up the ghost.' If we walk in those same footsteps in Jesus Christ, we also will have life uninterrupted. We can't halfway live as He did or halfway believe His Word; live in Christ today or a couple of hours on Sunday and the rest of the day we are in the world. This is what brings death. Jesus gave His all. We are also required to give our all.

John 5:39 Search the scriptures; for in them ye think ye have eternal life: and they are they which testify of me.

Here Jesus is talking to the religious men of that day. They thought they really knew the scriptures; but, they did not, otherwise they would have recognized who he was. Why? Because the scriptures they knew described Him and His purpose.

1 Cor. 15:53-54 For this <u>*corruptible*</u> **must** <u>*put on incorruption,*</u> *and this* <u>*mortal*</u> **must** <u>*put on immortality.*</u> *So when this corruptible shall have put on incorruption, and this mortal shall have put on immortality, then shall be brought to pass the saying that is written, Death is swallowed up in victory.*

Corruptible means: decayed, perishable. *Mortal* means: liable to die. *Put on* means: in the sense of sinking into a garment; to invest with clothing, clothe with. *Incorruptible* means: unending existence, un-decayed.

Our soulish nature or our emotions and our intellect brings

death to our bodies. This nature is changed by the Spirit of God that dwells in us. It is changed and brought back under subjection to the incorruptible spirit of Christ in us. We 'put on' the name or nature of Christ. As we walk more and more in the nature of Christ, the death nature that is in us is being swallowed up by Him, causing this mortal (that that is capable of dying, the body) to change into immortal. We cannot defeat death if we physically die. We are the one that has been defeated. We must fulfill the saying: Death is swallowed up in victory. This says 'put on' the garment not take it off. If we die, we are taking off the garment. As we are changed inwardly, we will begin to see a change outwardly.

2 Tim. 1:10 But is now made manifest by the appearing of our Saviour Jesus Christ, who hath abolished death, and hath brought life and immortality to light through the gospel:

What was abolished? Death. What was brought to light? Life and immortality. You notice the scripture did not say spiritual life or death, just life or death.

2 Cor. 4:11 For we which live are alway delivered unto death for Jesus' sake, that the life also of Jesus might be made manifest in our mortal flesh.

Study *2 Cor. 5.* It will give you an insight into life and immortality. The epistles are written about it. This is what Jesus did. He reversed the curse of death that was placed on Adam and restored life once again to mankind. We need to arouse ourselves from death, shake off the dust of the earth, and live.

2 Cor. 5:4 For we that are in this tabernacle (body) do groan, being burdened (by death): not for that we would be unclothed (die), but clothed (live) upon, that mortality (capable of dying) might be swallowed up of life.

The more Christ reigns in your body, the more life you will have. What happens when He is ruling and reigning 100% from his throne in you?

LET'S REVIEW:

1. What is being restored according to *Psalm?*

2. What does the word 'restore' mean?

3. When was the soul lost?

4. What does the separation of the spirit and soul bring and why?

5. Give examples of things that the locust, the cankerworm, and the palmerworm have destroyed.

6. What does 'perish' mean?

7. What does 'eternal' mean?

8. What does 'life' mean?

9. According to *1 John 5:11*, what is the record or evidence given?

10. How do we get eternal life?

11. What is His flesh?

12. What is His blood?

13. Explain 'raise him up at the last day.'

14. What is given to those who continue to seek patiently?

15. What does 'immortality' mean?

16. What makes you decay?

17. What are the wages or payment of sin?

18. What is the gift of God?

19. If God is eternal life and He dwells in us, what is in us?

20. Who cannot lie?

21. What was promised before the world began?

22. Through whom was life manifested before us?

23. What did the religious men of that day think they had?

24. What MUST put on incorruption?

25. What does 'incorruption' mean?

26. What does 'corruptible' mean?

27. What does 'mortal' mean?

28. What does 'immortal' mean?

29. What does 'put on' mean?

30. What brings death to our bodies?

31. How is the soulish nature changed?

32. What is to be swallowed up?

33. Where does the change begin?

34. Who abolished death?

35. Then, why are we still dying?

36. What was brought to light?

37. How was it brought to light?

38. Where is the life of Jesus to be manifested?

39. Who reversed the curse of death?

40. What happens when Christ is ruling and reigning 100% from his throne in you?

NOTES:

† Chapter 8 †

Kingdom of God

For years, we have waited to die to go to heaven to live and enjoy the benefits of the Kingdom of God; but, *Luke 17:21* says the Kingdom of God is within you. That tells me, then, I can live out of the Kingdom now. We need to realize what and who we are and begin to live out of our true identity now, not sometime after we die. We have been living an alias: *AKA* Adam.

Scripture says Jesus was the last man Adam, *I Cor. 15:45-50*. My flesh might have been born after Adam, but thanks to Jesus Christ, my spirit was born after His likeness and image.

2 Cor. 5:17 Therefore if any man be in Christ, he is a new creature: old things are passed away; behold, all things are become new.

Gal. 3:27 For as many of you as have been baptized into Christ have put on Christ.

Eph. 4:24 And that ye put on the new man, which after God is created in righteousness and true holiness.

Col. 1:13 Who hath delivered us from the power of darkness, and hath translated us into the kingdom of his dear Son:

Now, if we have realized that Christ has rescued us and carried us over to His kingdom, how do we live from there?

John 4:24 God is a Spirit: and they that worship him must worship him in spirit and in truth.

It says God is *A* Spirit, which means there are others. What are you?

I Cor. 15:44 It is sown a natural body; it is raised a spiritual body. There is a natural body, and there is a spiritual body.

2 Cor. 5:1 For we know that if our earthly house of this tabernacle were dissolved, we have a building of God, an house not made with hands, eternal in the heavens.

Gal. 3:27 For as many of you as have been baptized into Christ have put on Christ.

Eph. 4:24 And that ye put on the new man, which after God is created in righteousness and true holiness.

You sowed that natural body through baptism, which left what? A spiritual body. Our problem is we keep digging up the old body and trying to wear it again, but it stinketh. You cannot put new wine in old wine bottles *(Matt. 9:17)* .

To know God and to commune with Him, we must do it from

the spirit that we are. After you truly realize that you are spirit clothed in skins, then you can begin to worship him in Spirit and in Truth.

Worship: Meaning to kiss, like a dog licking his master's hand; to fawn or crouch to; prostate oneself in homage; do reverence to, adore.

Matt. 6:33 But seek ye first the kingdom of God, and his righteousness; and all these things shall be added unto you.

Seek means to worship God. Worship or adore or revere God and His justice, and, everything else will fall into place. We are seeking backwards.

Matt. 16:25 For whosoever will save his life shall lose it: and whosoever will lose his life for my sake shall find it.

Worship Him in spirit and in truth. The religious factions and even his disciples would ask Jesus a question. Every time, Jesus would answer their questions spiritually; but, they would always receive it with a natural understanding. He spoke in parables for a reason.

Matt. 13:34-35 All these things spake Jesus unto the multitude in parables; and without a parable spake he not unto them: That it might be fulfilled which was spoken by the prophet, saying, I will open my mouth in parables; I will utter things which have been kept secret from the foundation of the world.

We must always hear God's word from the Spirit to know its truth; but, the religious world is still always interpreting it carnally. God is Spirit and you must hear Him spiritually. This is what Jesus told them:

Mark 1:14-15 Now after that John was put in prison, <u>Jesus</u> came into Galilee, preaching the gospel of the kingdom of God, And saying, The <u>time</u> is fulfilled, and the kingdom of God is at hand: repent ye, and believe the gospel.

Who was the time? Jesus had fulfilled the scriptures. They had all pointed to Him and His coming. How was the Kingdom of God at hand? What Jesus was about to accomplish would usher in the age of grace. What did He do besides die on the cross for our sins?

Rev. 1:18 I am he that liveth, and was dead; and, behold, I am alive for evermore, Amen; and <u>have</u> the <u>keys</u> of <u>hell</u> and of <u>death</u>.

Jesus told the Jews to repent or change their religious way of thinking and believe the gospel or the word that he was teaching. Jesus was telling them about the truth of where the Kingdom was, what it was, how to live out of it and what its benefits were. He was telling them that His death on the cross would restore back to man what Adam had lost in the garden, life. He wasn't referring to spiritual life.

Rom. 12:2 And be not conformed to this world (ORDERLY ARRANGEMENT OF THINGS, SOCIETY AS IT IS): but be ye transformed (METAMORPHOSED, TRANSFIGURED, CHANGED) by the renewing of your mind, that ye may prove what is that good, and acceptable, and perfect, will of God.

Remember, Jesus was transfigured or metamorphosed on the mount. This gives us a picture of receiving our experience of the third feast, Tabernacles.

Col. 3:10-14 And have put on the new man, which is renewed in knowledge after the image of him that created him: Where there is neither Greek nor Jew, circumcision nor uncircumcision, Barbarian, Scythian, bond nor free: but Christ is all, and in all. Put on therefore, as the elect of God, holy and beloved, bowels of mercies, kindness, humbleness of mind, meekness, long-suffering; Forbearing one another, and forgiving one another, if any man have a quarrel against any: even as Christ forgave you, so also do ye. And above all these things put on charity, which is the bond of perfectness.

The new man is renewed in knowledge after the image of God. How does the new man get the renewed knowledge? By the hearing of the word and the revealing of it by the Holy Spirit. As you hear the word by the spirit and apply it to your life, you will see a mind set changed. You will begin to look more like the creator every day and less like the creature. It is not found in a religious doctrine or in the keeping of laws other than the law of the Spirit; nor does your gender or nationality matter. You are known by who you are in the Spirit.

1 Cor. 15:53-54 For this corruptible must put on incorruption, and this mortal must put on immortality. So when this corruptible shall have put on incorruption, and this mortal shall have put on immortality, then shall be brought to pass the saying that is written, Death is swallowed up in victory.

Physical death cannot be swallowed up in victory as long as man is still physically dying. Religion teaches that this has to do with spiritual death. Your spirit does not die nor has it ever died. It was or is held captive in darkness. Jesus brought those held captive, even those disobedient in the days of Noah, *out into His mar-*

101

velous light (Eph. 4:8-10, 1 Peter). Jesus defeated or rendered death inactive in Him. He showed us how and made the way for us to follow Him and be overcomers. Jesus was an overcomer on this side of death or He could not have faced what He did on the cross and in death and come out victorious.

Luke 9:23 And he said to them all, If any man will come after me, let him deny himself, and take up his cross daily, and follow me.

You are to take up your cross DAILY. You are to follow Him DAILY. Daily means you would have to do it on this side, not in death.

Rev. 2:7 He that hath an ear, let him hear what the Spirit saith unto the churches; To him that overcometh will I give to eat of the tree of life, which is in the midst of the paradise of God.

Hear what He is saying by the Spirit, not by the traditions of men. Jesus operated out of the spirit to deal with the natural and existed right here, living and operating in both realms. We are to follow Him. Aren't we coming after Him? He gave us the pattern to follow. He's the Tree of Life and that Tree of Life is in the midst of the garden, in the midst of us, our spirit. We are the paradise of God. If we eat of Him, scripture says we will LIVE! It didn't say you will live after you die. It says you will live. I believe what the Word says.

Rev. 2:17 He that hath an ear, let him hear what the Spirit saith unto the churches; To him that overcometh will I give to eat of the hidden manna, and will give him a white stone, and in the stone a new name (nature) written, which no man knoweth saving he that receiveth it.

There is a hidden word that can only be found by the spirit. That hidden word will change your nature. It cannot be imitated. It will be a pure, undefiled word.

Rev. 3:21 To him that overcometh will I grant to sit with me in my throne, even as I also overcame, and am set down with my Father in his throne.

Where is the seat or throne of God? In us. If we overcome the flesh, we can sit with Him as Kings and Priests of this House (our body, soul and spirit) and rule with Him.

LET'S REVIEW:

1. According to the scriptures, where is the Kingdom of God?

2. When can you start living out of the Kingdom of God?

3. What is our true identity?

4. If you are in Christ, you are a new what?

5. Where were we translated at our deliverance or repentance?

6. Who was the last man Adam?

7. If Jesus was the last man Adam, and, we were born after Him, what does that make us?

8. How did you sow the natural body?

9. What is your earthly house?

10. What is our house not made with hands?

11. With what is our true identity clothed?

12. We are to worship God in our true identity or in what?

13. How do you lose your life? Does this mean to naturally die?

14. How do you find your life?

15. Why did Jesus speak in parables?

16. Jesus told them this was fulfilled through Him and this was at hand or right in front of them.

17. Who was the time?

18. What kept them from seeing and hearing?

19. What age was Jesus ushering through His death, burial and resurrection?

20. What does repent really mean?

21. How are we changed or transformed?

22. When does this change or transformation begin to take place?

23. Where and when was Jesus transfigured?

24. How is the new man renewed? After what?

25. What is the elect of God to put on?

26. When we don this, what image will we reflect?

27. What must we put on to be fully clothed?

28. What does corruptible mean?

29. What does incorruptible mean?

30. What does mortal mean?

31. What does immortal mean?

32. Scripture says you are to not take it off (die).

33. What must we defeat on this side for death to be swallowed up in victory?

34. What was His cross besides the sins of the world? What did He have to defeat?

35. How often are we to take up His cross?

36. According to *Rev. 2:7*, it will take this to understand what God is saying to us.

37. *Rev. 2:7* also says if you do this you will eat of the tree of LIFE.

38. Who is the tree of LIFE?

39. Where does the overcoming take place and what are you to overcome?

40. Where is this tree of LIFE?

41. Who is the paradise of GOD?

42. To eat of Life, we would then have to do what?

43. Where is the throne of Christ?

44. If you die, there is one less throne from where Christ can rule and reign. Why would He want to sit on our throne and rule and reign?

45. Why did Jesus pray, 'Thy **Kingdom COME** on *Earth* as it is in *Heaven*'?

46. If you were going 'off' to Heaven, why would Jesus pray that it *COME HERE?*

47. Why would you need it here?

48. Who is the earth?

49. Jesus said He was bringing Heaven and earth together, in Him; therefore, He is bringing body and spirit together in Him to rule and reign where?

NOTES:

† *Chapter 9* †

The Bride

The church has taught that Christ is **GOING TO RETURN** for a Bride; but, let's take a long, intense look at the scriptures and see if it is future tense.

Rom. 8:18-19 For I reckon that the sufferings of this present time are not worthy to be compared with the glory which shall be revealed in us. For the earnest expectation of the creature waiteth for the manifestation of the sons of God.

Revealed means to take off the cover, disclose. We need to begin to ask 'What glory?' is to be revealed in us.

Earnest expectation means intense anticipation. *Waiteth* means to expect fully. The Creature or creation, with intense anticipation, expects fully the disclosure or appearing of the **sons of God.** Who are the sons of God? A son is produced from a union.

When Jesus came 2,000 years ago, He established the Kingdom of Heaven right here. John the Baptist told the people to repent that the Kingdom of Heaven *IS* (present tense), not will be. This is because Jesus was on the scene. He was the Kingdom of Heaven or the ruler of that realm brought here through Him. In *Matt. 4:17,* Jesus even began to preach, 'Repent, for the Kingdom of Heaven is at hand.' The day God announced that Jesus was His only begotten Son, it was settled. Jesus then received power and began doing miracles, establishing the Kingdom.

While studying for a lesson, God revealed to me by the scripture in *Col. 1:12-21* that the dispensation of Grace and the dispensation of Kingdom were both established at the same time. We have been looking for the dispensation of Kingdom to come, when it has been here all along. We couldn't see it because Grace overshadowed it. The more you fulfill the age of Grace, the more you begin to see the age of Kingdom and realize its presence.

The witness of who Jesus was to the apostles was seen on Mount Transfiguration, with Moses and Elijah, who represented the Law and the Prophets.

Matt. 16:28-17:3 Verily I say unto you, There be some standing here, which shall not taste of death, till they see the Son of man coming in his kingdom. And after six days Jesus taketh Peter, James, and John his brother, and bringeth them up into an high mountain apart, And was transfigured before them: and his face did shine as the sun, and his raiment was white as the light. And, behold, there appeared unto them Moses and Elias talking with him.

Peter, James, and John witnessed Jesus experiencing his tabernacles or **BEING CHANGED.** This established His Kingdom on earth.

Acts 1:11 Which also said, Ye men of Galilee, why stand ye gazing up into heaven? this same Jesus, which is taken up from you into heaven, shall so come in like manner as ye have seen him go into heaven.

In what form was Jesus when He went away? Spirit. Two thousand years ago, Jesus' second coming happened 50 days later in the upper room when He appeared as spirit and fell on them as the Holy Ghost. People are still looking for His return and He has been here all along, but, in another form.

*Luke 17:20-21 And when he was demanded of the Pharisees, when the kingdom of God should come, he answered them and said, The kingdom of God cometh not with observation: Neither shall they say, Lo here! or, lo there! for, behold, the kingdom of God is **within you.***

To show you that Jesus and the Holy Ghost are the one and the same, just different manifestations, read the following scriptures slowly and carefully. We tend to read scriptures according to how we have been doctrinally taught over the years, thus, missing the truth.

Matt. 3:11 I indeed baptize you with water unto repentance: but he that cometh after me is mightier than I, whose shoes I am not worthy to bear: he shall baptize (fully immerse) you with the Holy Ghost, and with fire:

John 14:6 Jesus saith unto him, I am the way, the truth, and the life: no man cometh unto the Father, but by me.

*John 14:16-19 And I will pray the Father, and he shall give you another Comforter, that he may abide with you for ever, Even the Spirit of truth (*which is whom? Jesus*): whom the world cannot receive, because it seeth him not, neither knoweth him: but ye know him; for he dwelleth <u>with</u> you, and shall be <u>in</u> you. <u>I will not leave you comfortless: I will come to you</u>. Yet a little while, and the world seeth me no more (*as Jesus*); but ye see me (*as you experience me as the Holy Ghost*): because I live, ye shall live also.*

*John 14:26 But the Comforter, which is the Holy Ghost, whom the Father will send in my name (*nature*), he shall teach you all things, and bring all things to your remembrance (*that I have taught you*), whatsoever I have said unto you.*

*John 14:28-29 Ye have heard how I said unto you, <u>I go away</u>, and <u>come again unto you</u>. If ye loved me, ye would rejoice, because I said, I go unto the Father: for my Father (*spirit*) is greater than I (*spirit*). And now I have told you before it come to pass, that when it is come to pass, ye might believe.*

Acts 1:5 For John truly baptized with water; but ye shall be baptized with the Holy Ghost not many days hence.

Jesus told the apostles this before His ascension so that they would recognize Him when He came in another form, Spirit. They knew Him after the flesh and were to know Him after the Spirit.

2 Cor. 5:16 Wherefore henceforth know we no man after the flesh: yea, though we have known Christ after the flesh, yet now henceforth know we him no more.

Acts 2:1-4 And when the day of Pentecost was fully come, they were all with one accord in one place. And suddenly there came a sound from heaven as of a rushing mighty wind, and it filled all the house where they were sitting. And there appeared unto them cloven tongues like as of fire, and it sat upon each of them. And they were all filled with the Holy Ghost, and began to speak with other tongues, as the Spirit gave them utterance.

This is the union or marriage that took place to begin producing **Sons of God.** The early church was born, salvation took place. With the baptism of the Holy Ghost, the bride conceives and produces the **Word.** We are becoming the Word, Sons of God. The apostles received the Word. It was birthed in them. When I say birthed in them, I mean, the Word became alive to them through the experience of it. The Word, therefore, became the Truth to them. They, in turn, gave the Word; then, it began to produce. The twelve apostles became the twelve loaves of shew bread that was found in the tabernacle. They broke themselves as bread to feed the spiritually hungry.

Acts 2:41 Then they that gladly received his word were baptized: and the same day there were added unto them about three thousand souls.

Acts 2:43 And fear came upon every soul: and many wonders and signs were done by the apostles.

They reproduced what Jesus Christ produced.

Acts 2:46-47 And they, continuing daily with one accord in the temple, and breaking bread from house to house, did eat their meat with gladness and singleness of heart, Praising God, and having favour with all the people. And the Lord added to the church daily such as should be saved.

Rev. 12:1-6 And there appeared a great wonder in heaven; a woman clothed with the sun, and the moon under feet, and upon her head a crown of twelve stars: And she being with child cried, travailing in birth, and pained to be delivered. And there appeared another wonder in heaven; and behold a great red dragon, having seven heads and ten horns, and seven crowns upon his head. And his tail drew the third part of the stars of heaven, and did cast them to the earth: and the dragon stood before the woman which was ready to be delivered, for to devour her child as soon as it was born. And she brought forth a man child, who was to rule all nations with a rod of iron: and her child was caught up unto God, and his throne. and the woman fled into the wilderness, where she hath a place prepared of God, that they should feed her there a thousand two hundred and threescore days (1260 days: Ezek. 4:6 and Num. 14:34 -- God told Israel he would give them a day for a year).

The early church, the bride, was about to produce the Word of Life, or a Son Child, and the enemy was waiting to devour it. The early church went into the dark ages until the reformation of the Church with Martin Luther who saw the revelation of the Just shall live by Faith.

God was married to Israel. That union produced Christ. When we accept Christ as our Savior, we become His bride; but, don't stop there. You must begin to produce as the married wife or you will taste of death. When you begin producing the Word, you then become a son of God. We cannot say we are a son of God unless we have first been a wife, otherwise we are bastard sons.

John 1:12 But as many as received him, to them gave he power to become the sons of God, even to them that believe on his name:

Received means to **ACTIVELY** take or get hold of rather than passively to have offered to one. This word is something you are going to have to actively grasp hold of to receive the power or privilege **TO BECOME** a produced child or son of God. Sonship isn't just going to happen to you.

*Rom. 8:14 For as many as are **led** by the Spirit of God, they are the sons of God.*

One of the definitions that best fits for LED is *drive.* For as many as are driven by the Spirit of God, they are the sons of God.

I John 3:1-2 Behold, what manner of love the Father hath bestowed upon us, that we should be called the sons of God: therefore the world knoweth us not, because it knew him not. Beloved, now are we the sons of God, and it doth not yet appear what we shall be: but we know that, when he shall appear, we shall be like him; for we shall see him as he is.

Appear means to render apparent or manifest outwardly. We are NOW the sons of God, because we are reproducing after His likeness. It is not APPARENT to us yet what we shall be; but, when he is manifested outwardly or is apparent in us, we shall be like him or in his image.

*Rev. 1:5-6 And from Jesus Christ, who is the faithful witness, and the first begotten of the dead, (*first begotten means there will be others to follow, us*) and the prince of the kings of the earth. Unto him that loved us, and washed us from our sins in his own blood, and hath made us kings and priests unto God and his Father; to him be glory* *and dominion for ever and ever. Amen.*

*Rev. 5:9-10 And they sung a new song, saying, Thou are worthy to take the book, and to open the seals thereof: for thou wast slain, and hast redeemed us to God by thy blood out of every kindred, and tongue, and people, and nation; And hast made us unto our God kings and priests: and **we shall reign on the earth.***

Rev. 21:7 He that overcometh shall inherit all things; and I will be his God, and he shall be my son.

Christ was the testator. We are the heirs. If we die, we no longer can be heir. Heir is the one left living. We have to be married to Christ and produce LIFE. This is our FULL inheritance. If death takes us, we cannot inherit ALL things.

Heb. 2:10 For it became him, for whom are all things, and by whom are all things, in bringing many sons unto glory (full manifestation),

LET'S REVIEW:

1. What glory shall be revealed in us?

2. What does 'earnest expectation' mean?

3. What does 'waiteth' mean?

4. Who is the creature?

5. For what is the creature waiting?

6. Who are the sons of God?

7. The kingdom of heaven is where?

8. When did John the Baptist say it would come?

9. What did Jesus begin to preach?

10. Where was the witness of who Jesus was revealed?

11. What two gave witness of who He was and what did they represent?

12. What three apostles witnessed Jesus experiencing His tabernacles?

13. What form was Jesus in when He went away?

14. When did the second coming of Jesus take place?

15. In what form was He?

16. Jesus said, 'The Kingdom of God cometh not with' what?

17. In what will Jesus immerse you?

18. Jesus said He would not leave you comfortless, but, would come to you how?

19. He said He would go away and come again unto you; and, He did. When?

20. What union took place to begin producing sons of God?

21. As the bride, what are we to be producing?

22. If you do not produce as the married wife, you will taste of what?

23. If you are not married to Christ first, you are a son of a what?

24. What does 'received' mean?

25. What does 'led' mean?

26. When does Paul say we are the sons of God?

27. What does 'appear' mean?

28. How will He appear?

29. Through the washing of His blood, what has Jesus made us?

30. Where shall we reign?

31. Who is the testator?

32. Who is the heir?

33. What will we inherit?

34. What must we do to inherit ALL things?

35. Christ is bringing many sons unto what?

NOTES:

Chapter 10

Clouds of Glory

In chapter 4, I briefly covered clouds. I would like to take just a moment to reiterate what I brought on clouds. The only way you will see what Christ was truly preaching to the apostles is by seeing it through types and shadows.

Hebrews 10:1 clearly tells us that the law was a shadow or picture of good things to come, Christ in His Kingdom. *Hebrews 8:4-5* says that the priests that offered sacrifices daily were only a shadow pointing to the true sacrifice, Jesus. God told Moses to make the tabernacle exactly to a tee by the instructions He gave him. Why? It was a pattern of us, the true tabernacle, indwelled by the Spirit.

Hebrews 9:23-24 says Christ is not entered into the holy place made by man's hand, which was the figure of the true tabernacle.

2 Cor. 3:2-3 Ye are our epistle written in our hearts, known and read of all men: Forasmuch as ye are manifestly declared to be the epistle of Christ ministered by us, written not with ink, but with the Spirit of the living God; not in tables of stone, but in fleshy tables of the heart.

Here, we find that we are epistles or books. That would make us a type and shadow of the Word of God. When we see that natural things were used as patterns for heavenly things or things in the invisible, we can begin to see ourselves as the Clouds of Glory. We know that God led the children of Israel in the wilderness with a cloud by day and a pillar of fire by night. This was no coincidence. It was pointing toward something. We also saw God appearing in the tabernacle as a cloud. Let's find out of what clouds are types.

By looking at natural clouds, we see that they hold rain. Spiritually, what does rain represent? Spirit. Who holds the Spirit? We do. The natural sun shines through the clouds when they are transparent enough; but, sometimes, the clouds are so dense when they cover the sun that it keeps us from seeing the sun and its light. Who is our light? God is. What is light? The revelation of the word. Lightning also comes out of the clouds. What is lightning?

Luke 17:24 For as the lightning, that lighteneth out of the one part under heaven, shineth unto the other part under heaven; so shall also the Son of man be in his day.

Lightning means glare, bright shining, to flash. What happens when the light bulb comes on? You can see what you couldn't see in the darkness. Remember the -ing is progressive. Just as you do not see a flash of lightening, most usually, all at once, you will not see the full depth of God's Word all at one time. First, you see the starting point or the flash of lightening -- its progression -- then its ending or fullness. When lightning occurs, it lights up the sky or heavens and the earth. When spiritual lightening occurs, something in the Word is revealed to you.

Usually, lightning is accompanied by a loud clap of thunder. Your heavens are shaken. A great noise is heard in your heaven. What you thought you knew is exposed by the light to be something totally different. Did you ever see a scary shadow in the dark; and, when the light was turned on, it was something simple and harmless?

In chapter 4 according to *2 Peter* and *Jude*, we read that men were referred to as wells and clouds. Men without the Spirit of Christ. They were brute beasts. They were also referred to as trees, raging waves and wandering stars.

Hosea 13:2-3 And now they sin more and more, and have made them molten images of their silver, and idols according to their own understanding, all of it the work of the craftsmen: they say of them, Let the men that sacrifice kiss the calves. Therefore they shall be as the morning cloud, and as the early dew that passeth away, as the chaff that is driven with the whirlwind out of the floor, and as the smoke of the chimney.

We see, then, in Hosea that men are referred to as the morning cloud, chaff, and smoke.

Hosea 6:4 O Ephraim, what shall I do unto thee? O Judah, what shall I do unto thee? for your goodness is as a morning cloud, and as the early dew it goeth away.

Judah's goodness or nature was compared to a morning cloud that produces the early dew and then goes away. This tells me that Judah's nature had changed. What does it tell you?

Eze. 38:8-9 After many days thou shalt be visited: in the latter years thou shalt come into the land that is brought back from the sword, and is gathered out of many people, against the mountains of Israel, which have been always waste: but it is brought forth out of the nations, and they shall dwell safely all of them. Thou shalt ascend and come like a storm, thou shalt be like a cloud to cover the land, thou, and all thy bands, and many people with thee.

The people will be so great in number, they will be like a storm and a cloud covering the land.

Pro. 25:14 Whoso boasteth himself of a false gift is like clouds and wind without rain.

Who is the cloud and the wind without what? By now, we should be able to see that God used clouds to represent man. In the Old Testament, God traveled as a cloud or likened to a cloud to point to the New Testament, Christ traveling in clouds, US.

Gen. 9:13 I do set my bow in the cloud, and it shall be for a token of a covenant between me and the earth.

What is the bow? A rainbow has seven colors reflected through one as a prism: white. What do the seven colors represent? The spirits of the Lord. God was talking about a covenant between Him and the natural earth. Who is the earth? We are. What was the covenant? He was going to give us **Life**. He was giving us

120

Christ. Where does Christ dwell? In us, His clouds of glory.

Lev. 16:2 And the Lord said unto Moses, Speak unto Aaron thy brother, that he come not at all times into the holy place within the vail before the mercy seat, which is upon the ark; that he die not: for I will appear in the cloud upon the mercy seat.

Aaron couldn't go into the Holiest of Holies just any time he pleased. There was an appointed time for Him to enter behind the vail. The tabernacle is a picture of man -- **body, soul and spirit**. Where did God appear? In the Holiest of Holies in the cloud upon the Mercy Seat. Christ is seated in our spirit on the mercy seat. He has covered us by grace that we might be able to endure and over-come to see and partake of the Kingdom of God that resides within us.

Lev. 16:13 And he shall put the incense upon the fire before the Lord, that the cloud of the incense may cover the mercy seat that is upon the testimony, that he DIE not:

What was the testimony? That man die not. Do we believe the testimony? By what I see displayed by most Christians, NO. They think it is for after you die. How can you receive the testimony 'that he die not' if you are looking to die first?

Gal. 1:15-16 But when it pleased God, who separated me from my mother's womb, and called me by his grace, To reveal his Son IN me, that I might preach him among the heathen; immediately I conferred not with flesh and blood.

Where does it say the Son was revealed? In him.

2 Cor. 2:20 I am crucified with Christ: nevertheless I live; yet not

I, but Christ liveth <u>in</u> me: and the life which I now live in the flesh I live by the faith of the Son of God, who loved me, and gave himself for me.

Where does Christ live? Then keep Him there and quit trying to put Him back up in the natural sky.

Gal. 4:19 My little children, of whom I travail in birth again until Christ be FORMED <u>in</u> you,

Where will Christ be formed? In you!

2 Thes. 1:10 When he shall come to be glorified IN HIS SAINTS, and to be admired IN ALL them that believe (because our testimony among you was believed) in that day.

Where is He coming to be glorified? In His saints. Who are His saints? I am. You are. Where will He be admired or seen? In all that believe. If you can't see His coming in you as a saint, then you can't say you believe.

1 Thes. 4:17 Then we which are alive and remain shall be caught up together (with them) in the clouds, to meet the Lord in the air: and so shall we ever be with the Lord.

Remember, this is symbolic or a type and shadow. Caught up means to seize, take by force. Do we not get 'caught up' in the atmosphere or emotion surrounding ball games, weddings, births, funerals, etc.? The moment seizes us. When we leave the event, slowly, we return to what we call the norm of our lives; but, we are affected by where we have been and what we felt.

Meet means a friendly encounter. *Air* means to breathe, spirit.

If we are the clouds, according to every scripture we have read, where will we be seized? In our body, our soul and spirit. We that are alive are going to be seized or taken by force by the spirit of Christ and have an encounter with Him that will cause us to stay in His presence continually. We have experienced a down payment of this encounter through salvation and the baptism of the Holy Ghost.

*Luke 21:27 And then shall they see the Son of man coming in A CLOUD (*me or you*) with power and great glory.*

You notice in *1 Thes.* it was clouds, plural. Here, in Luke, He is coming in 'a' cloud, singular. Where will the son of man be seen? In each individual cloud. His power and great glory will be manifested and radiate out of each of us. We are to Christ as the rays are to the sun. You can't have the sun without the rays, nor the rays without the sun.

Mark 14:62 And Jesus said, I am: and ye shall see the Son of man sitting on the right hand of power, and coming in the clouds of heaven.

Who is the right hand of power? God. Who are the clouds of heaven? Christians.

Matt. 24:30 And then shall appear the sign of the Son of man in heaven: and then shall all the tribes of the earth mourn, and they shall see the Son of man coming in the clouds of heaven with power and great glory.

John 14:9 Jesus saith unto him, Have I been so long time with you, and yet hast thou not known me, Philip? he that hath seen the Fa-

ther; and how sayest thou then, Shew us the Father?

If the Father -- the creative spirit -- was in Jesus, and Jesus is being formed in us, where will we see Christ coming? I hope you said 'In US!' I don't know how to make it any plainer. If you can't see it now, either ask God to open your spiritual eyes and ears or get in the Word and prove me wrong -- not by what man has taught you -- but, by what you see. Most usually when you try to prove it wrong, it will open your eyes of understanding; because, what you thought it said according to man's teaching, it really doesn't.

LET'S REVIEW:

1. What was a shadow of good things to come?

2. What were the good things to come?

3. What was Moses to built exactly by the blueprints?

4. Of what was this a type?

5. We are epistles or what?

6. We are not written by ink but by the what?

7. How did God lead the children of Israel in the wilderness?

8. What do natural clouds hold?

9. What do spiritual clouds hold?

10. Who is our light?

11. What is light?

12. What is lightning?

13. The suffix -ing causes the word to mean what?

14. Spiritually, what does lightning do?

15. What does a loud clap of thunder do?

16. Name some of the examples used to refer to men being without the spirit.

17. The tabernacle is a picture of man in his entirety, which is?

18. In the tabernacle of Moses, where did God appear?

19. Where is Christ seated?

20. What was the testimony covered by the cloud on the mercy seat?

21. Paul says God called him to reveal what in him?

22. *2 Cor. 2:20* says Christ lives where?

23. According to *Gal. 4:19*, Christ is being formed where?

24. Where is Christ going to be glorified?

25. By whom will He be admired?

26. Who are His saints?

27. What does 'caught up' mean?

28. What does 'meet' mean?

29. What does 'air' mean?

30. Have you ever been temporarily caught up in the spirit?

31. Would you like to experience it permanently?

32. We are what to whom as rays are to the sun?

33. Who are the clouds of heaven?

34. Where will we see Christ coming?

NOTES:

† Chapter 11 †

Uncovering The Mystery

In chapter 2, I briefly touched on the mystery that has been reserved and hidden from mankind since the foundation of the world. It has been reserved for a specific generation *(1 Peter 2:9)*; the NOW generation. To prove more in depth that this is true, let's take a look at some of the many mysteries that God has for man.

2 Thes. 2:7 For the mystery of iniquity doth already work: only he who now letteth will let, until he be taken out of the way.

We need to know and understand the mystery concerning iniquity in order to deal with it. Otherwise, it will have its way in us until we are taken out of the way.

1 Tim. 3:16 And without controversy great is the mystery of godliness: God was manifest in the flesh, justified in the Spirit, seen of angels, preached unto the Gentiles, believed on in the world, received up into glory.

There is a mystery concerning godliness. A 'way' is set before us to follow. This is a road map; follow it. Step 1) How was He manifested in the flesh? Believe on Jesus; 2) Justified in the spirit? Receive the Holy Ghost; 3) Seen of angels? He brought a message. You must see the revelation; then, preach and adhere to it. Where will it take you spiritually? You will be seized and changed by Him because He is the Word.

1 Tim. 3:8-10 Likewise must the deacons be grave, not double-tongued, not given to much wine, not greedy of filthy lucre; Holding the mystery of the faith in a pure conscience. And let these also first be approved; then let them use the office of a deacon, being found blameless.

There is a mystery of faith. There is a key to unlock faith. How must it be held? In a pure conscience. That means no doubting, no mixture or compromise in your life.

1 Cor. 2:7 But we speak the wisdom of God in a mystery, even the hidden wisdom, which God ordained before the world unto our glory:

There is a mystery in the wisdom of God. *Ordained* means premeditate. When did God premeditate this mystery that was to be hidden for a particular time? What does 'world' mean? It means 'the orderly arrangement of things'. Our world or society as we know it today was not the same as it was 50, 100, 1000 years ago. Today, we have the 'world' of high finance; the world of sports, crime, porno, etc.

Glory is from a base word meaning 'to think' (among others), good pleasure. There is a mystery of wisdom that can only be found in God that was reserved for us before the orderly arrangement of things began. This wisdom is to take us to glory or His manifestation in us.

Ephes. 1:9 Having made known unto us the mystery of his will, according to his good pleasure which he hath purposed in himself:

There is a mystery of His will. What is it? Remember, we read above that glory means good pleasure. What He is doing will be good pleasure unto us or bring us to glory for His good pleasure or manifestation.

Mark 4:11 And he said unto them, Unto you it is given to know the mystery of the kingdom of God: but unto them that are without, all these things are done in parables:

We see a mystery of the Kingdom. The apostles were privileged to have the mystery of the Kingdom of God revealed to them. What was the mystery?

Rev. 10:7 But in the days of the voice of the seventh angel, when he shall begin to sound, the mystery of God should be finished, as he hath declared to his servants the prophets.

Has it been finished? Yes. Once it was finished it could be revealed. It was finished and revealed through Christ; but, you have to have an 'ear' to hear and 'eye' to see. This is what Jesus was always saying after His parables or responses to the people.

Col. 2:2-3 That their hearts might be comforted, being knit together in love, and unto all riches of the full assurance of understanding, to the acknowledgment (recognition or discernment) of the mystery of God, and (BOTH) of the Father, and of Christ; In whom are hid all the treasures of wisdom and knowledge.

How are we to be knit together? It is God's love that knits us together and will take us, if we will follow, unto all riches of UNDERSTANDING, ACKNOWLEDGMENT OF THE MYSTERY, WISDOM AND KNOWLEDGE.

These riches are found in the Father and Christ. The only way to get them is by going to God through Jesus Christ. Any other way is as a thief and robber.

Rom. 11:25 For I would not, brethren, that ye should be ignorant of this mystery, lest ye should be wise in your own conceits; that (spiritual) *blindness in part is happened to Israel, until the fulness of the Gentiles* (Christ crucified) *be come in.*

What has this mystery revealed? Not only did we see the natural grafting in of the Gentiles; but, what would 'Gentiles' represent in the spirit? Your flesh. What is Israel? Your spirit. Hasn't man's spirit denied Christ the same as Israel did? Our flesh or soulish nature must be brought in to inherit along with our spirit. It has to come back under subjection to the spirit of God. It has to be restored, as David said. Here's another mystery.

1 Cor. 15:51 Behold, I shew you a mystery; We shall not all sleep (to slumber or decease), *but we shall all be changed* (to make different),

What is the revelation? We will not all die, but, all will be made different. Do you feel you are changing now? Are you the same or will you stay the same? Do you believe the scriptures? If so, then, how could you ever question that He wants us to live and not die? Are we to know the mysteries? Yes!

Ephes. 3:3-4 How that by revelation he made known unto me the mystery; (as I wrote afore in few words, Whereby, when ye read, ye may understand my knowledge in the mystery of Christ)

We are to participate in the mystery.

Ephes. 3:8-11 Unto me, who am less than the least of all saints, is this grace given, that I should preach among the Gentiles the unsearchable riches of Christ; And to make (TO SHED RAYS) all men see (same word as make) what is the fellowship (partnership or participation) of the mystery, which from the beginning of the world hath been hid in God, who created all things by Jesus Christ: To the intent (purpose) that now unto the principalities and powers in heavenly places might be known by the church the manifold wisdom of God, According to the eternal purpose which he purposed in Christ Jesus our Lord:

We are to preach, to shed light, that all will see that we are to participate or be a partner in the mystery. What was the mystery here? To know the purpose of the chief magistrate and powerful influences in high places; that we would see His plan and purpose for the church.

Rom. 16:25 Now to him that is of power to stablish you according to my gospel, and the preaching of Jesus Christ, according to the revelation of the mystery, which was kept secret since the world began,

What was the revelation and preaching of the Anointed or Christ?

Col. 1:25-29 Whereof I am made a minister, according to the dispensation (administration or economy) of God which is given to me for you, to fulfil the word of God; Even the mystery which hath been hid from ages and from generations, but now is made manifest to his saints: To whom God would make known what is the riches (fullness) of the glory (good pleasure) of this mystery among the Gentiles; which is Christ (anointed) in you, the hope (to anticipate, expectation, or confidence) of (WHAT?) glory: Whom we preach, warning every man, and teaching every man in all wisdom; that we may present every man perfect in Christ Jesus: Whereunto I also labour, striving according to his working, which worketh in me mightily.

What was the mystery? The hope of glory is renaming Christ. The hope of glory or good is in you. The ability to think good as He does is in you. The anticipation and expectation or faith is in you. Where will it take you?

Rom. 8:11 But if the Spirit of him that raised up Jesus from the dead dwell in you, he that raised up Christ from the dead shall also quicken (make alive) your mortal bodies by his Spirit that dwelleth in you.

Is that good news? Once we have the understanding of the good news or the mysteries, what do we do with them besides apply them to our life?

Col. 4:3 Withal praying also for us, that God would open unto us a door of utterance, to speak the mystery of Christ, for which I am also in bonds:

Ephes. 6:19 And for me, that utterance may be given unto me, that I may open my mouth boldly, to make known the mystery of the gospel.

Jesus saw the mystery through the Spirit of God dwelling in Him. He preached it to the apostles. After His resurrection or standing up again, through the Holy Ghost, the mystery was re-vealed to them and they began to preach it and proclaim it throughout the land. When we see the mystery of LIFE revealed, we are to open our mouths BOLDLY when God opens a door for us and proclaim the mystery that not all shall sleep or die, but, all shall be changed or made different -- be made unto His image.

LET'S REVIEW:

1. What has been reserved and hidden from mankind from the foundation of the world?

2. List some of the mysteries mentioned in the scriptures.

3. How do you unlock the mystery of faith?

4. When did God premeditate the mystery of wisdom?

5. Where will this mystery of wisdom take us?

6. What was the mystery of the Kingdom?

7. What are the treasures hidden in the Father and Christ?

8. He showed us a mystery concerning the Gentiles. What was it?

9. *1 Cor. 15:51* shows us a mystery concerning LIFE. What is it?

10. We are to know the mysteries of God. Why has He kept them hidden until now?

11. Why were the Pharisees and Sadducees not able to see them?

12. What did you have to have to be able to see and understand the mysteries?

13. What spirit raised Jesus from the dead?

14. Does that same spirit dwell in you? If so, what will it do for you?

15. What are we to do with the mystery when we see it?

NOTES:

† Chapter 12 †

End of The World

All my life I have heard people talk about the world coming to an end. As a child, I would be afraid to go to sleep at night for fear the world would come to an end and I wouldn't be able to hold on to my parents when it happened. It is a shame that the church world, through ignorance of the scriptures, placed this kind of horrible fear in its people, especially children. They even placed fear in me through a bed time prayer: Now I lay me down to sleep. If I should DIE before I wake, I pray the Lord my soul to take. Now do you see why I was afraid to go to sleep at night? I was afraid I would die in my sleep. I praise God daily for His truth and the revealing of His Word to me. I now can go to bed at night knowing I have LIFE dwelling in me.

The scriptures, if studied, plainly tell us what the 'end of the world' is. Man's theology by the works of the enemy or the carnal mind (which is enmity against God) has clouded the truth. The first place to start is to find the meaning of 'world'. According to Strong's Concordance, it means the orderly arrangement of things. *Webster's Dictionary* says it is human society, any domain or activity. Remember the movie *Wayne's World*? What did that mean? It was Wayne's way of social life. The word 'end' means something concludes and something new begins.

Gen. 6:13 And God said unto Noah, The end of all flesh is come before me; for the earth is filled with violence through them; and behold, I will destroy them with the earth.

God didn't say He would destroy the earth along with them; but, he used the earth or nature's measures to bring them to ruin. We know the earth didn't come to an end because we are still walking and living on it. The world or society as Noah knew it in his region was destroyed by nature's force, a flood. If God was going to destroy the earth, why would He have told Noah to build the ark?

Gen. 9:11 And I will establish my covenant with you; neither shall all flesh be cut off any more by the waters of a flood; neither shall there any more be a flood to destroy the earth.

Why never a flood again? A flood, as we well know, tears up and utterly destroys where ever it flows. God is using the flood as a shadow of heavenly things, because we still see natural floods today. What do the flood waters represent? The cleansing power of His spirit. It will either lift you up, if you are of it, or, will purge you if you are not.

Deut. 28:49 The Lord shall bring a nation against thee from far, from the end of the earth, as swift as the eagle flieth; a nation whose tongue thou shalt not understand;

We see from the above scripture that 'end of the earth' is used as a figure of speech. We know there is no literal end or edge of the earth. Man discovered years ago that the earth was not flat.

Psa. 19:6 His going forth is from the end of the heaven, and his circuit unto the ends of it: and there is nothing hid from the heat thereof.

Do you think that heaven has come to an end?

Psa. 37:37-38 Mark the perfect man, and behold the upright: for the end (result or way) of that man is peace. But the transgressors shall be destroyed together: the end (way) of the wicked shall be cut off.

Psa. 46:9 He maketh wars to cease unto the end of the earth; he breaketh the bow, and cutteth the spear in sunder; he burneth the chariot of the fire.

Psa. 61:2 From the end of the earth will I cry unto thee, when my heart is overwhelmed: lead me to the rock that is higher than I.

Can you see that the phrase 'end of the earth' is used figuratively, not literally? The rock that is higher than me is Jesus Christ.

Eze. 7:3 Now is the end come upon thee, and I will send mine anger upon thee, and will judge thee according to thy ways, and will recompense upon thee all thine abominations.

Eze. 7:6 An end is come, the end is come: it watcheth for thee; behold, it is come.

The end, if you are looking for it, has already come. Jesus Christ was THE END. He brought an end to the old creature and made us a new creature in Him. He brought an end to the age of LAW and brought a new age, GRACE.

Matt. 5:5 Blessed are the meek: for they shall inherit the earth.

If God was going to destroy the earth, why would He say the meek are going to inherit it? Would you want an inheritance that was going to be destroyed?

Matt. 13:47-50 Again, the kingdom of heaven is like unto a net, that was cast into the sea, and gathered of every kind: Which, when it was full, they drew to shore, and sat down, and gathered the good into vessels, but cast the bad away. So shall it be at the end of the world: the angels shall come forth, and sever the wicked from among the just, And shall cast them into the furnace of fire: there shall be wailing and gnashing of teeth.

Psa. 104:35 Let the sinners be consumed out of the earth, and let the wicked be no more. Bless thou the Lord, O my soul. Praise ye the Lord.

The kingdom of heaven is not a kingdom in the sky somewhere. Jesus was telling them that the world or society as they knew it was coming to an end. The dispensation of Law was ending and grace was beginning. What did we just read in *Psa. 104*? It's not the earth that is to be destroyed; but, the 'way' that we live our life, if it is not in God, it will be consumed.

Matt. 28:20 Teaching them to observe all things whatsoever I have commanded you: and, lo, I am with you alway, even unto the end of the world. Amen.

The world of Law ended on the cross. Jesus was with them until it ended.

Rom. 10:4 For Christ is the end of the law for righteousness to every one that believeth.

1 Cor. 15:24 Then cometh the end, when he shall have delivered up the kingdom of God, even the Father; when he shall have put down all rule and all authority and power.

Jesus Christ put down all rule and all authority and power, including death, in His resurrection. The end came.

Heb. 9:26 For then must he often have suffered since the foundation of the world: but now once in the end of the world hath he appeared to put away sin by the sacrifice of himself.

1 Peter 1:13 Wherefore gird up the loins of your mind, be sober, and hope to the end for the grace that is to be brought unto you at the revelation of Jesus Christ;

Rev. 2:26 And he that overcometh, and keepeth my works unto the end, to him will I give power over the nations.

If the world was coming to an end, why would God give you power over something that was not here? We wouldn't be here to be given the power, let alone, use it. We have been told that the earth was once destroyed by water and the next time it would be utterly destroyed by fire.

Luke 12:49 I am come to send fire on the earth; and what will I if it be already kindled?

Matt. 3:11 I indeed baptize you with water unto repentance: but he that cometh after me is mightier than I, whose shoes I am not worthy to bear: he shall baptize (totally immerse) you with the Holy Ghost, and with fire:

Heb. 12:29 For our God is a consuming fire.

That fire is God and I am His earth. I am totally immersed in Him and He is burning up everything in me that is not of Him: all envy, strife, hatred, fornication, uncleanness, idolatry, etc. *(Gal. 5:17-21)*. His fire will burn until the only thing left is love, joy, peace, long-suffering, gentleness, goodness, faith, meekness, temperance. The only thing you will see left in me is HIM. The scripture says you will not see Jesus come again until you can say blessed is he that cometh in the name (nature) of the Lord. You will see Him again through mankind when they manifest His nature. He came once as a man and is coming again as a many membered man where He is the head.

LET'S REVIEW:

1. What is the meaning of 'world'?

2. What is *Webster's* meaning for 'world'?

3. How did God destroy all flesh in *Gen. 6*?

4. Why never a flood again?

5. What do the flood waters represent?

6. How is 'end of the earth' used?

7. What does *Psa. 19:6* say has come to an end?

8. In *Psa. 37,* what does the word 'end' mean?

9. If you can see it, who was the end?

10. How was He the end?

11. According to *Matt. 5,* what are the meek going to inherit?

12. Where did the 'world' of Law end?

13. What did Christ put down in His resurrection?

14. If you are an overcomer, what will you receive?

15. Who is the fire and who is the earth?

16. What is to be consumed in us?

17. What will be left?

18. How will you see the coming of Jesus Christ?

19. Through whom will you see Him?

NOTES:

[†] *Chapter 13* [†]

Heaven or Hell?

This will probably be the toughest chapter I will write. Why? Because, the concept of hell has absolutely been burned into our minds since Greek mythology. If you will listen to the conversation of most Christians, they are condemning someone to rot in hell. I've already covered what and where heaven is. Through this chapter, I hope to shine light on the truth about the origin and meaning of 'hell'.

Greek and Roman mythology, along with *Dante's Towering In-ferno* and *Milton's Paradise Lost,* has infiltrated religion. A literal burning hell, as we have been taught, came out of these writings. Fire was never associated with the devil in the Bible. It was always associated with God. Words like -- fire, outer darkness, grave, devil -- are associated with hell. Let's take these words and prove their true meaning by the scriptures.

DARKNESS

Gen. 1:2 And the earth was without form, and void; and darkness was upon the face of the deep. And the Spirit of God moved upon the face of the waters.

Gen. 1:4-5 And God saw the light, that it was good: and God divided the light from the darkness. And God called the light Day, and the darkness he called Night. And the evening and the morning were the first day.

Darkness means (literal) darkness; (figurative) misery, destruction, ignorance, sorrow, wickedness.

The earth, or mankind, was without form and void. *Form* means to lie waste; a desolation, i.e. desert; a worthless thing; confusion, empty place, without form, nothing, (thing of) naught, vain, vanity, waste, wilderness. *Void* means to be empty; a vacuity, i.e. (superficially) an indistinguishable ruin: emptiness, void.

Face represents the direction you are going or what you see and understand, naturally or spiritually. *Deep* means water-supply (spirit). *Light* means to be (causative make) luminous (literal and metaphorical), break of day, glorious, kindle, (be, en-, give, show) light (-en, -ened) set on fire, shine. *Be enlightened.*

Stated simply, mankind was desolate, in a confused state, and ignorant of God. God moved upon man's spirit (made man a living soul -- gave him intellect that would be ruled by 5 senses or emotions) and brought enlightenment of Himself to man. When man began to follow his own intellect or emotions instead of following God, he fell.

When you receive a revelation and its understanding, you are no longer in darkness of it, but, walking in the light or day of it. God rebukes Israel's unjust judges for showing partiality to the wicked and not showing justice to the weak, fatherless, afflicted and destitute. He says of the people:

Psa. 82:5 They know not, neither will they understand; they walk on in darkness: all the foundations of the earth are out of course.

We know the earth does not have 'foundations'. The people are ignorant of His plan and purpose, and because of their ignorance, they are out of course or line with Him.

*Psa. 107:10 Such as sit in darkness and in the shadow of death, being bound in affliction and iron (*judgment*);*

Death, as used in the above scripture, means 'the grave.' His people were sitting in ignorance of Him which was keeping them in bondage, placing them in the shade of the grave or headed for death.

Psa. 107:14 He brought them out of darkness and the shadow of death, and brake their bands in sunder.

Job talks about being in a place of ignorance concerning God.

Job 10:21-22 Before I go whence I shall not return, even to the land of darkness and the shadow of death; A land of darkness, as darkness itself; and of the shadow of death, without any order, and where the light is as darkness.

Job 12:22 He discovereth deep things out of darkness, and bringeth out to light the shadow of death.

Job 17:12-13 They change the night into day: the light is short because of darkness. If I wait, the grave is mine house: I have made my bed in the darkness.

Grave means Hades or the world of the dead (as if a subterranean retreat), including its accessories and inmates: grave, hell, pit. Notice that the word grave means hell? I am not making up these definitions. Look them up for yourself in *Strong's Exhaustive Concordance of the Bible.*

2 Cor. 4:6 For God, who commanded the light to shine out of darkness, hath shined in our hearts, to give the light of the knowledge of the glory of God in the face of Jesus Christ.

What are our hearts? Our minds. Where do we conceive God or the devil? In our minds, right? The scripture tells us to put on the mind of Christ. He dispelled the ignorance and enlightened us of what? God has given us the truth of who and what His glory is through the face or direction that Jesus Christ walked.

2 Cor. 6:14 Be ye not unequally yoked together with unbelievers: for what fellowship hath righteousness with unrighteousness? and what communion hat light with darkness?

How can you converse or walk with someone, be it your spouse, friend, etc., if you have been enlightened to what God is doing in this day and the other has not? It brings confusion and contention between the two.

Matt. 6:23 But if thine eye be evil, thy whole body shall be full of darkness. If therefore the light that is in thee be darkness, how great is that darkness!

Matt. 8:12 But the children of the kingdom shall be cast out into outer darkness: there shall be weeping and gnashing of teeth.

When people read this scripture, they think the backsliders are going to be thrown into hell. If darkness is ignorance, to me, this says that those that are Christians that are ignorant of the truth will really be upset when the light dawns.

Ephes. 5:8 For ye were sometimes darkness, but now are ye light in the Lord: walk as children of light:

Remember we read in *Genesis* that God divided the light from the darkness and called the light *Day* and the dark *Night*. *Ephesians* says we were *sometimes* darkness, but now, we are *light*. We are to walk or live according to what we know in God.

1 Thes. 5:4-5 But ye, brethren, are not in darkness, that that day should overtake you as a thief. Ye are all the children of light, and the children of the day: we are not of the night, nor of darkness.

This clearly tells us who the light and day and the night and darkness are.

Isa. 45:7 I form the light, and create darkness: I make peace, and create evil: I the Lord do all these things.

John 1:5 And the light shineth in darkness; and the darkness comprehended it not.

When Jesus walked among the Jews, he was the light shining in the darkness. They were the chosen people of God (*Matt. 8:12*) but they were in spiritual darkness and did not recognize who He was. They missed their day of visitation.

1 John 1:5-6 This then is the message which we have heard of him, and declare unto you, that God is light, and in him is no darkness at all. If we say that we have fellowship with him, and walk in dark-ness, we lie, and do not the truth:

KEEP THE ABOVE SCRIPTURE IN MIND.

FIRE

We have discovered that the light is the revealing of God's Word and the darkness is being spiritually ignorant of it. Next, we must understand who and what the fire is.

Gen. 3:24 So he drove out the man; and he placed at the east of the garden of Eden Cherubim, and a flaming sword which turned every way, to keep the way of the tree of life.

Flaming means a blaze; also from the idea of enwrapping - magic (as covert); flaming, enchantment, set on fire, kindle. Man-kind has been believing enchantments now for 2,000 years. *Covert* means to cover up or hide the truth. *Sword* means drought, also, a cutting instrument from its destructive effect, as a knife, sword, or other sharp implement; to parch, to desolate, destroy, kill.

What was placed to keep the way? Who put it there? God placed a fire that would bring a spiritual drought to man or a word that would parch or destroy anything that was not Godlike. This sharp word kept the way or entrance back to the tree of life.

Heb. 4:12 For the word of God is quick, and powerful, and sharper than any two-edged sword, piercing even to the dividing asunder of soul and spirit, and of the joints and marrow, and is a discerner of the thoughts and intents of the heart.

Only the purified will be able to pass by the flaming sword un-scathed and enter back into 'The Way' of the tree of life.

John 14:6 Jesus saith unto him, I am the way, the truth, and the life: no man cometh unto the Father, but by me.

To get back to the Father, you have to pass by that flaming sword: Christ, the Word. You will never get there any other way. The scripture says if you try, you are the same as a thief and a robber.

Gen. 19:24 Then the Lord rained upon Sodom and upon Gomorrah brimstone and fire from the Lord out of heaven;

Fire means burning, fiery, fire, flaming, hot. What did we see placed in the garden? The *flaming* sword.

Ex. 3:2 And the angel of the Lord appeared unto him in a flame of fire out of the midst of a bush: and he looked, and behold, the bush burned with fire, and the bush was not consumed.

Ex. 13:21 and the Lord went before them by day in a pillar of a cloud, to lead them the way; and by night in a pillar of fire, to give them light; to go by day and night:

Ex. 19:18 And mount Sinai was altogether on a smoke, because the Lord descended upon it in fire: and the smoke thereof ascended as the smoke of a furnace, and the whole mount quaked greatly.

Ex. 24:17 And the sight of the glory of the Lord was like devour-

ing fire on the top of the mount in the eyes of the children of Israel.

Ex. 40:38 For the cloud of the Lord was upon the tabernacle by day, and fire was on it by night, in the sight of all the house of Israel, throughout all their journeys.

As you can see, by all these scriptures in the Old Testament, God used fire in dealing with the people. He used it to consume the people's sacrifices as a symbol of purifying and purging flesh (carnal nature).

Lev. 9:24 And there came a fire out from before the Lord, and consumed upon the altar the burnt offering and the fat: which when all the people saw, they shouted, and fell on their faces.

God destroyed Israel's enemies and their cities with fire.

Deut. 4:33 Did ever people hear the voice of God speaking out of the midst of the fire, as thou hast heard, and live?

Deut. 4:36 Out of heaven he made thee to hear his voice, that he might instruct thee: and upon earth he shewed thee his great fire; and thou heardest his words out of the midst of the fire.

2 Sam. 22:9 There went up a smoke out of his nostrils, and fire out of his mouth devoured: coals were kindled by it.

2 Kings 2:11 And it came to pass, as they still went on, and talked, that behold, there appeared a chariot of fire, and horses of fire, and parted them both asunder; and Elijah went up by a whirlwind into heaven.

Dan. 3:25 He answered and said, Lo, I see four men loose, walking in the midst of the fire, and they have no hurt; and the form of the fourth is like the Son of God.

Acts 2:3 And there appeared unto them cloven tongues like as of fire, and it sat upon each of them.

2 Thes. 1:7-8 And to you who are troubled rest with us, when the Lord Jesus shall be revealed from heaven with his mighty angels, in flaming fire taking vengeance on them that know not God, and that obey not the gospel of our Lord Jesus Christ:

Man began to defile the purpose of fire just as they have defiled the Word of God.

Lev. 10:1-2 And Nadab and Abihu, the sons of Aaron, took either of them his censer, and put fire therein, and put incense thereon, and offered strange fire before the Lord, which he commanded them not. And there went out fire from the Lord, and devoured them, and they died before the Lord.

2 Kings 17:17 And they caused their sons and their daughters to pass through the fire, and used divination and enchantments, and sold themselves to do evil in the sight of the Lord, to provoke him to anger.

2 Kings 17:31 And the Avites made Nibhaz and Tartak, and the Sepharvites burnt their children in fire to Adrammelech and Anammelech, the gods of Sepharvaim.

2 Kings 21:6 And he (Manasseh, king of Judah) made his son pass through the fire, and observed times, and used enchantments, and dealt with familiar spirits and wizards: he wrought much wickedness in the sight of the Lord, to provoke him to anger.

*Isa. 54:16 Behold, I have created the smith that bloweth the coals in the fire, and that bringeth forth an instrument (*vessel, tool, weapon*) for his work; and I have created the waster to destroy.*

If you have not deduced by now who the fire is, here are some more clues.

Isa. 66:16 For by fire and by his sword will the Lord plead with all flesh: and the slain of the Lord shall be many.

Jer. 20:9 Then I said, I will not make mention of him, nor speak any more in his name. But his word was in mine heart as a burning fire shut in my bones, and I was weary with forbearing, and I could not stay.

Jer. 23:29 Is not my word like as a fire? saith the Lord; and like a hammer that breaketh the rock in pieces?

Dan. 10:6 His body also was like the beryl, and his face as the appearance of lightning, and his eyes as lamps of fire, and his arms and his feet like in colour to polished brass, and the voice of his words like the voice of a multitude.

This is all symbolic in describing our powerful God.

Deut. 4:24 For the Lord thy God is a consuming fire, even a jealous God.

Matt. 3:10-12 And now also the axe is laid unto the root of the trees: therefore every tree which bringeth not forth good fruit is hewn down, and cast into the fire. I indeed baptize you with water unto repentance: but he that cometh after me is mightier than I, whose shoes I am not worthy to bear: he shall <u>baptize</u> you <u>with the Holy Ghost</u>, and *with fire: Whose fan is in his hand, and he will thoroughly purge his floor, and gather his wheat into the garner; but he will burn up the chaff with unquenchable (perpetual) fire.*

Who's the fire? God. What's the chaff? Anything in us that is not Christ like. The Holy Ghost fire of God or the Anointed Word will not stop burning until all chaff is burned.

Matt. 13:40 As therefore the tares are gathered and burned in the fire; so shall it be in the end of the world.

1 Cor. 3:13 Every man's work shall be made manifest (good or bad): for the day shall declare it, because it shall be revealed by fire; and the fire shall try every man's work of what sort it is.

1 Cor. 3:15 If any man's work shall be burned, he shall suffer loss: but he himself shall be saved; yet so as by fire.

Did you just hear what God said? The man's work, if it is not of God, will be destroyed but the man himself will be saved! We always thought if man wasn't good, he was forever destroyed. He didn't have a chance in hell — figuratively speaking — but, now we know he does.

Heb. 12:29 For our God is a consuming fire.

By now, it should be *EXTREMELY* clear that the people knew and associated fire with God. It was not associated with the devil. Fire can be used to bring life or death, destruction. With this disclosure, you should be asking yourself, 'Then, what about hell?' Good question. But, before we discuss hell, let's find out about the grave, then, hell won't be so hard to understand.

GRAVE

There are various meanings and usage of the word 'grave.'

Gen. 35:20 And Jacob set a pillar upon her grave: that is the pillar of Rachel's grave unto this day.

The word *grave* here means a sepulcher, burying place. The Hebrew word is qebuwrah. I'll refer to it as sepulcher.

Gen. 37:35 and all his sons and all his daughters rose up to comfort him; but he refused to be comforted; and he said, For I will go down into the grave unto my son mourning. Thus his father wept for him.

Grave, as used here, means Hades or the world of the dead (as if a subterranean retreat), including its accessories and inmates: grave, hell, pit. It does not say for good or bad people, just world of the dead. Grave is also referred to as hell or a pit. In the Hebrew, it is called she'owl. In the following scriptures, I will indicate which definition is used: sepulcher or she'owl.

Gen. 44:29 And if ye take this also from me, and mischief befall him, ye shall bring down my gray hairs with sorrow to the grave. (She'owl)

Gen. 50:5 My father made me swear, saying, Lo, I die: in my grave which I have digged for me in the land of Canaan, there shalt thou not bury me. Now therefore let me go up, I pray thee, and bury my father, and I will come again. (Sepulcher)

Another use of grave is a Hebrew word, pathach, which means to open wide, to loose self, to (en)grave(-n), opening.

Ex. 28:36 And thou shalt make a plate of pure gold, and grave upon it, like the engravings of a signet, HOLINESS TO THE LORD. (Pathach)

1 Sam. 2:6 The Lord killeth, and maketh alive: he bringeth down to the grave, and bringeth up. (She'owl)

Job 5:26 Thou shalt come to thy grave in a full age, like as a shock of corn cometh in his season. (Sepulcher)

Job 7:9 As the cloud is consumed and vanisheth away: so he that goeth down to the grave shall come up no more. (She'owl)

Job 14:13 Oh that thou wouldest hide me in the grave, that thou wouldest keep me secret, until thy wrath be past, that thou wouldest appoint me a set time, and remember me! (She'owl)

Job 24:19 Drought and heat consume the snow waters: so doth the grave those which have sinned (miss the mark). *(She'owl)*

Grave is used yet another way. As the Hebrew word *shachath*, it means a pit (especially as a trap); to sink; figurative - destruction: corruption, destruction, ditch, grave, pit.

Psa. 6:5 For in death there is no remembrance of thee: in the grave who shall give thee thanks? (She'owl)

Death means die, the dead, their place or state (Hades); figurative - pestilence, ruin. Plainly speaking, in the realm of the dead, you can not give God thanks.

Psa. 30:3 O Lord, thou hast brought up my soul from the grave: thou hast kept me alive, that I should not go down to the pit. (She'owl)

This scripture almost sounds like double talk. David says 'He restoreth my soul.' If your soul is your emotions and intellect, governed by your five senses, God would not restore them *AFTER* you were dead. You wouldn't need them. When we allow ourselves to be ruled by our soul instead of by the spirit of Christ, it will bring death to us or take us to the grave. The word *pit* means a pit hole (especially one used as a cistern or prison): cistern, dungeon, fountain, pit, well. God, through Jesus Christ, has brought us up out of prison or the grave. Why are we still going there? We are still going there because of darkness or ignorance of the Word. We have listened to words of enchantment and they have kept the word covert or hidden, thus, producing death.

Psa. 31:17 Let me not be ashamed, O Lord; for I have called upon thee: let the wicked be ashamed, and let them be silent in the grave. (She'owl)

Silent means to be dumb; to be astonished, to stop, to perish; rest, tarry, wait. Let the wicked tarry or wait in the grave or death. Read *Rev. 20* and keep in mind the second death. We will cover it later.

Psa. 49:14 Like sheep they are laid in the grave, death shall feed on them; and the upright shall have dominion over them in the morning; and their beauty shall consume in the grave from their dwelling. (She'owl)

Beauty means a form, as if pressed out, carved, hence an idolatrous image. Believe it or not, because of religion, we have an image carved out in our mind of God. We, along with that image, shall be consumed by death. The word *sin* means miss the mark, come short of the glory of God. We sin every day or miss the mark as long as we follow after a graven image of God. The wages (payment) of sin is DEATH. We have come short of the glory of God or walking in LIFE. We have missed out on our FULL inheritance.

Psa. 49:15 But God will redeem my soul from the power of the grave: for he shall receive me. (She'owl)

Through Christ, God has ransomed or released us from the power or direction of the grave, death. *2 Tim. 1:10* says that Jesus Christ has abolished death and brought life and immortality to light through the gospel. We read this as meaning that after death we have life and immortality. Your spirit is already immortal because it came from God.

Rom. 8:11 But if the Spirit of him that raised up Jesus from the dead dwell in you, he that raised up Christ from the dead shall also quicken (make alive) *your MORTAL bodies by his Spirit that dwelleth IN you.*

Does that spirit dwell in you? If so, what will it quicken or make alive? Your immortal spirit? No, your MORTAL body.

Eccel. 9:10 Whatsoever thy hand findeth to do, do it with thy might; for there is no work, nor device, nor knowledge, nor wisdom, in the grave, whither thou goest. (She'owl)

What ever you are going to do, give it everything you've got because everything in this life that you thought was more important than God is worthless, if death overtakes you. It will be of no use to you in death.

Isa. 38:18 For the grave cannot praise thee, death can not celebrate thee: they that go down into the pit cannot hope for thy TRUTH. (She'owl)

This alone should be enough to prove to you that God does not want you to die. When you die, that is one less vessel for Him to dwell in on this earth. One less vessel to praise him, and, one less vessel to manifest the truth.

Eze. 31:15-17 Thus saith the Lord God; In the day when he went down to the grave I caused a mourning; I covered the deep for him, and I restrained the floods thereof, and the great waters were stayed: and I caused Lebanon to mourn for him, and all the trees of the field fainted for him. I made the nations to shake at the sound of his fall, when I cast him down to hell (death) *with them that descend into the pit* (death): *and all the trees of Eden, the choice and best of Lebanon, all that drink water, shall be comforted in the nether parts of the earth. They also went down into hell with him unto them that be slain with the sword* (word); *and they that were his arm, that dwelt under his shadow in the midst of the heathen.*

This is symbolic. God is comparing Egypt's destruction to that of Adam's. Because of Adam's ignorance or innocence, he lost LIFE. We really can't hold it against him, because it was in the plan and purpose of God.

Romans 8:20 says the creature (man) was made subject (obedient) to vanity (empty, idol), not willingly, but by reason of God. Adam or mankind did not have a choice until he was given one.

Hosea 13:14 I will ransom them from the POWER of the grave (death); *I will redeem them from death: O death, I will be thy* *plagues; O grave, I will be thy destruction: repentance shall be hid from mine eyes. (*She'owl*)*

What is going to happen to the grave? God is going to destroy it. The grave or hell can be on this side (life) or that (death). Your physical body is placed in a grave or sepulcher or can become a grave. Your spiritual body can be contained in a spiritual grave (death or Hades, the realm of the dead) on this side (your physical body) or the other side.

Matt. 23:27 Woe unto you, scribes and Pharisees, hypocrites! for ye are like unto whited sepulchers, which indeed appear beautiful outward, but are within full of dead men's bones, and of all uncleanness.

*John 19:41-42 Now in the place where he was crucified there was a garden; and in the garden a new (*freshness with respect to age*) sepulcher, wherein was never man yet laid. There laid they Jesus therefore because of the Jew's preparation day; for the sepulcher was nigh at hand.*

Jesus was laid in a tomb where no man had yet laid. Jesus was ushering in a new day or age, Grace, and destroying the hold of death and the grave. No man had been there before.

1 Cor. 15:55 O death, where is thy sting? O grave, where is thy victory?

Grave is the Greek word haides and means the place or state of departed souls: grave, hell. This is from where the word 'Hades' came. You notice it said place or state of departed souls. It did not say the soul of sinners.

Each time the Hebrew word 'She'owl' or the Greek word 'Hades' was used in the scriptures, it meant the same: death, hell, grave, pit. It is time to search out the word 'hell' and see what is revealed. Erase your mind of the image of a literal place with a literal burning fire with little demons running around with pitchforks poking people.

HELL

People relate Abraham's bosom and paradise to heaven and consider it to be opposite of hell.

Luke 16:22-23 And it came to pass, that the beggar died, and was carried by the angels into Abraham's bosom: the rich man also died, and was buried; And in hell he lift up his eyes, being in torments, and seeth Abraham afar off, and Lazarus in his bosom.

This was one of Jesus' parables. It is symbolic of the spiritual. The rich man is the defiled priesthood that fared sumptuously off the tithes and offerings brought into the temple by the people. Read how the rich man was dressed then compare it to the description of the priests that served in the temple.

The beggar represented the children of Israel. They were spiritually starving to death. The priesthood had nothing to spiritually offer them. Abraham represents God.

The word *bosom* means a bay or creek. A bay is an inlet of a body of water (as the sea) usually smaller than a gulf. It is bordered by land. Keep this in mind when we discuss the lake of fire. Doesn't the Word talk about the river of life flowing out of us?

The word *hell* or haides in the Greek means the unseen, i.e. the place (state) of departed souls: -grave, hell.

John 1:18 No man hath seen God at any time; the only begotten Son, which is in the bosom (bay) of the Father, he hath declared him.

2 Cor. 12:4 How that he was caught up into paradise, and heard unspeakable words, which it is not lawful for a man to utter.

Paradise means a park, i.e. an Eden. *Para* means along side. Where was Adam? He was in paradise with God 'along side' Him. When Paul experienced God on the road to Damascus, he was caught up and saw the realm of life or light. The invisible, spiritual world runs parallel to the visible. The scripture says to speak, bring or manifest that which is invisible into the visible. Paul was not physically dead when he went to paradise.

Luke 23:43 And Jesus said unto him, Verily I say unto thee, To day shalt thou be with me in paradise.

Rev. 2:7 He that hath an ear, let him hear what the Spirit saith unto the churches; To him that overcometh will I give to eat of the tree of life, which is in the midst of the paradise of God.

The word *bosom* is not used in the Old Testament referring to a place in God. Paradise is not used at all. Paradise or light was not available to mankind again until Christ went into the realm of the dead. Through His death and resurrection, He brought light (spiritual understanding) and life to us, by rendering the state or condition of death inactive in Him.

Eph. 4:8-10 Wherefore he saith, When he ascended up on high, he led captivity captive, and gave gifts unto men. (Now that he ascended, what is it but that he also descend first into the lower parts of the earth? He that descended is the same also that ascended up far above all heavens, that he might fill all things.)

Acts 2:24 Whom God hath raised up, having loosed the pains of death: because it was not possible that he should be holden of it.

*Rev. 1:18 I am he that liveth, and was dead; and, behold, I am alive for evermore, Amen; and have the keys of hell (*hades, realm of the dead*) and of death.*

Jesus holds the keys to hell and of death. Should you want to go through death or hell, you will have to go to Him to get the keys. Here's more scripture to prove what hell is:

2 Sam. 22:6 The sorrows of hell compassed me about; the snares of death prevented me;

The word '*sorrows*' means a rope (as twisted), especially a measuring line; a district or inheritance; ruin, snare, coast. We already know the definition of hell. Death had snared him.

Amos 9:2 Though they dig into hell, thence shall mine hand take them; though they climb up to heaven, thence will I bring them down.

Do you know anyone or have you ever heard of anyone digging into hell as we know it? I know we dig graves? Do you know anyone that has literally climbed to heaven? I know we climb mountains, stairs, ropes, and trees. I know if things get rocky, I 'climb' into the spirit of God. He is my refuge, my sanctuary, my bay or safe haven.

The word *dig* means to force a passage, as by burglary; figuratively with oars: dig (through), row. If hell is really what we've been taught, how can we dig into it? If it were possible, then I'd do it and release those captive there. Do we realize that the doctrines we have accepted came from our forefathers 100 years ago? They most likely came from someone that could not read. They heard it from someone and passed it on. Surely, you have played that game and know how the story gets misconstrued. Instead of really considering what is being taught and asking questions or searching for ourselves, we have accepted the interpretation from a person who is most likely illiterate and couldn't read the scriptures for themselves.

Matt. 25:41 Then shall he say also unto them on the left hand, Depart from me, ye cursed, into everlasting fire, prepared for the devil and his angels:

This scripture tells me the fire (God) is prepared for the devil and his messengers.

2 Peter 2:4 For if God spared not the angels that sinned, but cast them down to hell, and delivered them into chains of darkness, to be reserved unto judgment;

If the word *angel* means messenger or pastor - to bring tidings, who was the first to know about God? It was Adam. Was he not the first to (miss the mark) sin against God? Was the punishment awarded not death? We have, hopefully, found that death and hell are the same word. The word *hell* in this scripture is the Greek word tartaroo which means the deepest abyss of Hades; to incarcerate in eternal torment: - cast down to hell. This sounds like there are levels in Hades. Not only are you damned, but you are double damned!

Psa. 9:17 The wicked shall be turned (retreat) into hell (death, grave), and all the nations that forget God.

It doesn't say the nations are wicked but they just forgot about their God. He is literally going to send them to a burning fire because they forgot?! As a Christian, how often do you forget to commune with Him? Remember, hell is not just for the wicked.

Psa. 16:10 For thou wilt not leave my soul in hell; neither wilt thou suffer thine Holy One to see corruption.

God has shown David that his seedline, Jesus, would not be bound by death or the grave. Mankind would be restored. The curse of Adam would be reversed through David's seedline as God had promised. If this was the literal hell we think it is, David says God is not going to leave him in it. Oh, is there a way out? Is it temporary?

Psa. 86:13 For great is thy mercy toward me: and thou hast delivered my soul from the <u>lowest</u> (womb) <u>hell</u>.

Psa. 139:8 If I ascend up into heaven, thou are there: if I make my bed in hell, behold, thou art there.

No matter where you are or in what condition, God is there. You cannot get away from God. You cannot even go to hell and get away from Him. He has delivered you even from the LOWEST hell, where you conceive and produce carnality.

Isa. 28:15 Because ye have said, We have made a covenant with death, and with hell are we at agreement; when the overflowing scourge shall pass through, it shall not come unto us: for we have made lies our refuge, and under falsehood have we hid ourselves.

Have you noticed that when you read about death in the scriptures, it is usually connected to hell?

Isa. 28:18 And your covenant with death shall be disannulled, and your agreement with hell shall not stand; when the overflowing scourge shall pass through, then ye shall be trodden down by it.

Did you realize that you had a covenant with death and an agreement with hell? Good news. That covenant has been disannulled and will not stand.

Jon. 2:2 And said, I cried by reason of mine affliction unto the Lord, and he heard me; out of the belly of hell cried I, and thou heardest my voice.

I thought Jonah was in the belly of the great fish. This scripture says he was in the belly of hell. Had he not been delivered from his demise, the belly of the fish would have become his grave.

Matt. 5:22 But I say unto you, That whosoever is angry with his brother without cause shall be in danger of the judgment: and whosoever shall say to his brother, Raca, shall be in danger of the council: but whosoever shall say, Thou fool, shall be in danger of hell fire.

Hell used in the above scripture is the Greek word for geenna, which means valley of Hinnom; Gehenna, a valley of Jerusalem, used (figurative) as a name for the place (or state) of everlasting punishment: -hell. Remember Gehenna is where they were passing their children through the fire as sacrifices to the gods.

The scripture says you will be accountable for every idle word. *Proverbs 18:21* says the tongue holds the power of death and life. Every word produces something. You can either produce life or you can produce death by the words that proceed out of your mouth. Jesus said He did not live by bread alone, but, by every word that proceeded out of His mouth. He spoke the Word of God and it produced life for Him. He didn't have to depend on natural things to sustain Him. *Proverbs 15:4* says a wholesome tongue is a tree of life. On the other hand, scripture says the tongue is a flaming fire of iniquity.

James 3:6 And the tongue is a fire, a world of iniquity: so is the tongue among our members, that it defileth the whole body, and setteth on fire the course of nature; and it is set on fire of hell.

Matt. 10:28 And fear not them which kill the body, but are not able to kill the soul: but rather fear him which is able to destroy both soul and body in hell. (Gehenna)

Matt. 16:18 And I say also unto thee, That thou art Peter, and upon this rock I will build my church; and the gates of hell shall not prevail against it. (Haides)

The entrance to hell or death could not prevail or overpower the church if it was founded on the rock or foundation based on Jesus Christ concerning life and immortality. Death or the grave has prevailed for so long that it is hard to change the mind set. How long did it take the old timers to accept the fact that we could go to the moon? I remember when they laughed and scoffed at the idea. They said it could never be done. July 20, 1969, Neil Armstrong stepped out of the spaceship, *APOLLO,* onto the moon. Today, it is a normal occurrence. (Notice the similarity of the name to Apollyon in *Rev. 9:11*)

Phil. 2:10 That at the name of Jesus every knee should bow, of things in heaven, and things in earth, and things under the earth.

Under means subterranean, i.e. infernal (belonging to the world of departed spirits). The definition says 'world of departed spirits', not sinners. Every knee should bow no matter where they are found: alive or dead, in light or in darkness.

Col. 1:20 And, having made peace through the blood of his cross, by him to reconcile all things unto himself; by him, I say, whether they be things in earth or things in heaven.

Eph. 1:10 That in the dispensation of the fullness of times he might gather together in one all things in Christ, both which are in heaven, and which are on earth; even in him:

Dispensation means administration of a household or estate; specially a (religious) "economy". Who is the dispensation of the fullness of times? Jesus Christ. He fulfilled all the scriptures. Now, take the Hebrew and Greek definitions of fire, hell, grave, and darkness and apply them to what is written about them in *Revelations*.

REVELATIONS 19 - 20

So many people are afraid of *Revelations*. We must remember it is a book of symbols and about 95% of it has already been fulfilled. You will find this out for yourself if you will study church history. It was fulfilled naturally when Rome fell. John the Revelator saw down through the ages of time of things to come. God also gave him a revelation of what would take place spiritually. Let's concentrate on chapters 19-20.

Rev. 19:17 And I saw an angel standing in the sun; and he cried with a loud voice, saying to all the fowls that fly in the midst of heaven, Come and gather yourselves together unto the supper of the great God;

Get out of your mind an angel with a halo and wings. *Angel* means message or messenger, a pastor. Jesus was a pastor or teacher of the Word. They called Him 'Rabbi.' He brought a message that dealt with the fowls. *Sun* represents God and *fowls* represent the devouring spirits that rob you of God's Word and blessings. These fowls are lies and images that are in your heavens.

Rev. 19:18 That ye may eat the flesh of kings, and the flesh of captains, and the flesh of mighty men, and the flesh of horses, and of them that sit on them, and the flesh of all men, both free and bond, both small and great.

Flesh represents your human nature or being carnally minded. *Kings* represents a foundation of power. *Captains and mighty men* are those under the rulership of this power. *Horses*, of course, represent the power of this rulership.

We see in this verse that all carnality will be consumed.

Rev. 19:19 And I saw the beast, and the kings of the earth, and their armies, gathered together to make war against him that sat on the horse, and against his army.

The beast is man in his un-regenerated state. Man has a beastly nature without God. Religion has taught us that there would be a natural war of *Armageddon*. Where were the fowls called to eat? In the heavens. Where do you perceive God? In your mind. The true war of *Armageddon* is your carnal nature warring against the Christ nature in you. This war goes on daily and has since the fall of man. Where does the enemy talk to you? He talks to you in your mind or thoughts. Where does God talk to you? God talks to you in your mind or thoughts. Now, where is this war taking place?

Rev. 19:20 And the beast was taken, and with him the false prophet that wrought miracles before him, with which he deceived them that had received the mark of the beast, and them that worshipped his image. These both were cast alive into a lake of fire burning with brimstone.

From where did the beast come?

Rev. 17:8 The beast that thou sawest was, and is not; and shall ascend out of the bottomless pit, and go into perdition: and they that dwell on the earth shall wonder, whose names were not written in the book of life from the foundation of the world, when they behold the beast that was, and is not, and yet is.

Notice, John is told the beast he sees is not yet, but will be. I think He saw the age of technology. God unlocked man's imagination and the inventions began to pour out, the beast ascended. From where did it come? It came out of the depths of man's mind, son of perdition, -- good or bad -- and operated out of man's fleshly nature. Do we not marvel and gasp at the great things man continues to devise? Take a look at the horrid things the beast nature does to each other? There is no bottom or a foundation based on Christ that comes out of the mind of man. We know that Christ is *The Book of Life. Not written* represents all those that are without the nature of Christ.

A prophet is one who comes telling something. The *false prophet* represents the lies we are told by the enemy. Religion has tried to tag the *mark of the beast* on anything that comes along -- computers, computer chips, bar codes, satellites, -- or anyone with influence. Religion is looking in all the wrong places. You need to look only as far as your nose. The mark of the beast in the forehead is where the beast nature of man rules in the mind.

*Rev. 13:18 Here is **WISDOM**. Let him that hath understanding count the <u>number</u> of the <u>beast</u>: for it is the <u>number</u> of a <u>man</u>; and his number is six hundred threescore and six.*

The first thing the scripture says is 'WISDOM.' Wisdom in interpreting what the spirit is saying. Man is made up of three parts. Count them: ***body, soul, and spirit***. The scripture plainly says it is the number of A man, not a specific man. God's number is seven: Completeness, spiritual perfection. Man has fallen short of that number in his flesh, in his soul, and in his spirit. We worship the image of our flesh. Are we not always giving into it and trying to satisfy its demands? We worship the image of our soul. We are ruled by our intellect and emotions. We worship the image of our spirit. We have believed religious lies and fight anyone that tries to tell us differently.

Cast means to eject. Where were the beast and false prophet dwelling? They will be ejected out of the mind of man. Why alive? If the lies were dead, we wouldn't be in the shape we are now, nor would they need to be ejected. *Alive* means they are producing. *Lake* means through the idea of the nearness of shore; a pond; a harbor or haven.

When studying the bosom of Abraham, we found that it meant bay or God. A lake is surrounded by land, a place of safety. The land contains the water. Scripture tells us that God is a consuming fire. This lake was of fire. Put all this together and you will see that the *lake of fire* is God. *Burning* means to set on fire, i.e. kindle or consume; burn, light. When God burns out things in us that is not of Him, it brings the light or revelation.

Brimstone means sulphur; flashing, godlike, divine, godhead. God, being the lake and a consuming fire, will burn up anything not Godlike, producing (spiritual) (en)light(enment). The substance of the fire is divine or God. Where will the beast and false prophet be cast? Into God. Can we let go of our 'devilish' images and let them be consumed by God?

Rev. 20:1 And I saw an angel come down from heaven, having the key of the bottomless pit and a great chain in his hand.

Key means a clue or answer, a powerful word. Who has the keys? There is a message or word from God that will unlock the bottomless pit, or, the mind of man that is not founded on Christ.

Rev. 1:18 I am he that liveth, and was dead; and, behold, I am alive for evermore, Amen; and have the keys of hell and of death.

Christ holds the answer or a powerful word to hell and death. To find it, you need to realize the bottomless pit is not a literal place of a literal burning fire.

Rev. 9:1-2 And the fifth angel sounded, and I saw a star fall from heaven unto the earth: and to him was given the key of the bottomless pit. And he opened the bottomless pit; and there arose a smoke out of the pit, as the smoke of a great furnace; and the sun and the air were darkened by reason of the smoke of the pit.

Rev. 9:11 And they had a king over them, which is the angel of the bottomless pit, whose name in the Hebrew tongue is Abaddon, but in the Greek tongue hath his name Apollyon.

Through man's intellectual awakening, it has caused a smoke screen to arise. Man can't see God because he gives himself all the glory. The sun (God) and the air (Spirit) were darkened because of the smoke. *Apollyon:* nature of a destroyer. The *chain* is a powerful word that will bind the enemy in our minds.

Rev. 20:2-3 And he laid hold on the dragon, that old serpent, which is the Devil, and Satan, and bound him a thousand years, And cast him into the bottomless pit, and shut him up, and set a seal upon him, that he should not deceive the nations no more, till the thousand years should be fulfilled: and after that he must be loosed a little season.

Notice where the dragon or the devil is cast. The **Word of Life and Immortality** will bind the enemy in our minds and we will begin to know the truth and will be able to walk in it. Why is he loosed for a little season? The scripture says we are tried for the Word's sake. Those born in LIFE will have to have that Word tried for it to stand true in them. The *thousand years* represents an age ruled sovereignly by Christ through us, His kings and priests.

We will be allowed to sit on the throne with Him, because, we are His thrones.

Rev. 20:4 And I saw thrones, and they sat upon them, and judgment was given unto them: and I saw the souls of them that were beheaded for the witness of Jesus, and for the word of God, and which had not worshipped the beast, neither his image, neither had received his mark upon their foreheads, or in their hands; and they lived and reigned with Christ a thousand years.

We are those thrones. *Souls* are those not following after the flesh or carnal nature and its power. *Beheaded* means losing their head or will and letting Christ be their head. Their will becomes the will of the Father. Those experiencing tabernacles or the *change* will become the measuring rod or judgment on the earth. Those measuring up will reign as kings and priests or manifesting the nature of Christ on the earth.

Rev. 20:6 And when the thousand years are expired, Satan shall be loosed out of his prison, and shall go out to deceive the nations which are in the four quarters of the earth, Gog and Magog, to gather them together to battle: the number of whom is as the sand of the sea. And they went up on the breadth of the earth, and compassed the camp of the saints about, and the beloved city: and fire came down from God out of heaven, and devoured them.

The enemy comes out in full force with lies and deceit; but God, the consuming fire within us, devours the lies.

*Rev. 20:10 And the devil that deceived them was cast into the lake of fire and brimstone, where the beast and the false prophet are, and shall be tormented day and night for ever and ever (*age, Messianic period).

Where was the devil cast? Who else is in there? If the devil is the ruler of 'hell', how can he be thrown into his own domain?

Rev. 20:11 And I saw a great white throne, and him that sat on it, from whose face the earth and the heaven fled away; and there was found no place for them.

We know God is the great white throne. He is in rulership in us.

Face means towards view, countenance, appearance, presence, fashion. We know *earth* represents our earthy or carnal nature; but, why would the heaven flee away, if we are suppose to be going there? We have been fashioned by religion. Our nature will flee and we will have His nature or appearance.

Rev. 20:12 And I saw the dead, small and great, stand before God; and the books were opened: and another book was opened, which is the book of life: and the dead were judged out of those things which were written in the books, according to their works.

Everyone is a book. Those alive, but dead in Christ, were opened. *The book* was not in the original text.

Translators added it. We are the other book of life. The living dead or those that are alive that have not received Christ are judged according to how they measure up to the standard or word of life that has been established in us.

There was a time that the horse and buggy were used as the main mode of travel. Along came trains, planes and automobiles. They set a standard by which the horse and buggy were measured. Which would you choose to use? Today, they are considered an antique item. Wonder why? The horse and buggy were judged by something greater and they fell short. Therefore, the horse and buggy had become virtually obsolete. Something greater had come on the scene to take its place.

Rev. 20:13 And the sea (multitudes or world) gave up the dead which were in it; and death and hell delivered up the dead which were in them: and they were judged every man according to their works.

Those that went by the way of the grave were judged. Did they run the race as Paul did, pressing on for the prize of the High Call-ing? The sea represents the multitudes or the world or those in spiritual darkness.

Rev. 20:14 And death and hell were cast into the lake of fire. This is the second death.

Where was death and hell cast? If hell was the lake of fire, it could not be cast into itself. Death and hell are conditions. They were consumed by God. Those that did not accept Christ on this side will find themselves cast into the lake of fire, or God, for a time of purifying. This is the second death. They died once unto darkness. Now, they will have no other choice but to die out to Christ, the second death. Whether we want to accept it or not, the concept called Purgatory has some truth to it. The ritual per-formed by those on this side does not affect it *(Psa. 49:7-8).* It is going to happen, period. Call it what you will. Scripture bears it out.

Rev. 20:15 And whosoever was not found written in the book of life was cast into the lake of fire.

How much plainer can God say it. He says He is the consuming fire and book of life. Anything in you that is not of His nature will be burned out by Him, whether it be on this side of death or on the other side of death.

Rev. 21:1 And I saw a new heaven and a new earth: for the first heaven and the first earth were passed away; and there was no more sea.

When you have experienced God in His fullness, you will have a new heavenly mind, not full of religious images, and a new earth, a body changed. No more sea or no one living out of their carnal mind.

Rev. 21:4 And God shall wipe away all tears from their eyes; and there shall be no more death, neither sorrow, nor crying, neither shall there be any more pain: for the former things are passed away.

You will no longer see your shortcomings. You will be living out of the Kingdom. The condition of Death has been consumed by the fire. You finally realize 'Adam' is dead; former things truly have passed away. It's out of your remembrance.

Rev. 21:8 But the fearful, and unbelieving, and the abominable, and murderers, and whoremongers, and sorcerers, and idolaters, and all liars, shall have their part in the lake which burneth with fire and brimstone: which is the second death.

You cannot get away from the fire of God. You will go through it on this side or the other. Do I believe in hell? Yes, but, not in the image of 'hell' which religion teaches. Why? God has opened my eyes. I do not want to experience the second death. I choose to be purged in Him on this side. I choose to walk in LIFE. I choose to render death inactive in me as Jesus did; that I might be able to say, "O death, where is thy sting? O grave, where is thy victory?" I want this vessel to live so it can sing the praises of my God. I want to be counted among the first fruit company that ushers in LIFE. I want to rule with Him as a king and priest. That Day is Today. Live and walk in the power of the Kingdom of God TODAY.

I hope my attempt at explaining the scriptures, by which they were revealed to me, has stirred your spirit. If nothing else, to get you to study the scriptures in order to prove me wrong.

I must share this story concerning my husband, John. When we were first married, he was a 'dyed in the wool', hard core Baptist. I was skeptical about marrying him, not because of love, but, because of our differences in the Word. God showed me time and again, John was the one; but, I wasn't so sure. When I tried to share this Word, John would refuse to hear it and say I was off into false doctrine. This only made me frustrated and him more alienated. I told him God put us together for him to hear this word and he said God put us together to get me back on the right track. Finally, I said, "You get in the scriptures to prove me wrong and I'll get in the scriptures to prove you wrong."

John began to study like he had never studied before. It was like we were both desperate to prove the other one wrong. God began to open the Word up to John like he had never seen it before. It took the Spirit of God to move on him, not me. I was only an instrument.

I got into the Word and studied like never before. My foundation got stronger and stronger until I became a teacher of the Word. Our challenge to each other produced a union so strong in Christ that the gates of hell can not prevail against it. Today, we walk equally yoked in the Word, who is Christ.

LET'S REVIEW:

1. Why is this the toughest chapter written?

2. What has infiltrated religion?

3. What words are associated with hell?

DARKNESS

4. In the *Strong's,* which is the best word to describe darkness?

5. What does form mean?

6. What was without form and void?

7. What does face represent?

8. What does deep mean?

9. What does light mean?

10. Putting the above definitions together, you get a simple statement, which is:

11. When God moved upon man's spirit, what did He give him?

12. What caused man to fall?

13. What brings you into the light of the 'day'?

14. In *Psa. 107:10,* what does death mean?

15. Where were His people?

16. What does Job talk about concerning the people and God?

17. What does grave mean?

18. What is our heart?

19. Where do we conceive God?

20. Where do we conceive the devil?

21. To what were we enlightened?

22. How did He give us the truth?

23. You were sometimes in darkness, but now you are?

24. How are you to walk?

25. According to *1 Thes. 5:4-5,* who is the light, darkness, day,

night?

26. Who formed the light, created the darkness, made peace, and created evil?

27. Who was the light walking among the Jews, shining in darkness?

28. Who was the darkness that did not recognize the light?

FIRE

29. What have we discovered that the spiritual light does?

30. What is the flaming sword in *Genesis 3?*

31. What was it to do?

32. Who is able to pass through the flaming sword?

33. What does fire mean?

34. How was fire used in the Old Testament?

35. How did man begin to defile the purpose of fire?

36. In *Jeremiah,* God says His word is like a what?

37. *Deuteronomy* says God is a _____ and a jealous God.

38. What is the chaff?

39. Who is going to burn the chaff?

40. How will man be saved?

41. What does *Hebrews 12:29* say about God?

42. The people knew and associated what with God?

43. When did fire begin to be associated with the devil?

GRAVE

44. Name the various meanings and usage of the word grave?

45. Where is no remembrance of God?

46. Who shall give God thanks if you are in this place?

47. What does the word death mean?

48. If we are ruled by our what, it will bring death to us and take us where?

49. God, through Jesus Christ, has brought us up out of what?

50. Why are we still going there?

51. What is keeping it hidden?

52. What is it producing?

53. What does silent mean?

54. Beauty means what?

55. What does the word sin mean?

56. What are the wages of sin?

57. God has ransomed us from the power of what?

58. What has Jesus Christ abolished and what has He brought to light?

59. What will His indwelling spirit do for you?

60. What cannot praise Him and cannot celebrate Him?

61. What caused Adam to lose LIFE?

62. To what did Jesus compare the scribes and Pharisees?

63. From where did the word Hades come?

64. To what does the word Hades refer?

HELL

65. To what do people relate Abraham's bosom?

66. Of whom is the rich man symbolic?

67. Of whom is the beggar symbolic?

68. What dispensation day or age did Jesus fulfill?

69. What day did He usher in for us?

70. What does the word hell mean?

71. What does the word paradise mean?

72. Where was Adam?

73. What does para mean?

74. When was Paradise or light made available?

75. Who has the keys to hell and death?

76. According to scripture, for whom is the fire prepared?

77. What does the word angel mean?

78. Who brought the curse of death?

79. Who would reverse it?

80. If you make your bed in hell, who is in there with you?

81. With what has the covenant been disannulled?

82. What agreement will not stand?

83. What did Jonah call the belly of the fish?

84. What does the Greek word geenna mean?

85. What is in the power of the tongue?

86. What does the word of God produce?

87. A wholesome tongue is what?

88. The tongue can also be a flaming fire of what?

89. To what could the entrance of hell not prevail?

90. What does the word under mean?

91. What does the word dispensation mean?

92. Who is the dispensation of the fullness of time?

REVELATIONS 19 - 20

93. *Revelations* is a book of what?

94. When was most of it fulfilled?

95. What did John the Revelator see?

96. What do the fowls represent?

97. What is the beast?

98. What does man have without God?

99. What war is going on in you?

100. Those who are 'not written' in the book of Life are who?

101. What is the bottomless pit?

102. Man is made up of what three parts?

103. How has man fallen short in all three parts?

104. Who is the lake of fire?

105. What is the bosom of Abraham?

106. Where will the beast and false prophet be cast?

107. What does the word key mean?

108. Who has the keys to the bottomless pit?

109. Why can't man see God?

110. What is the 'chain'?

111. Where is the dragon cast?

112. What will bind the enemy?

113. Why is he loosed for a little season?

114. What does the thousand years represent?

115. What does beheaded mean?

116. In *Rev. 20:10,* where was the devil cast?

117. Who else was in there?

118. What is the false prophet?

119. Who is the great white throne?

120. What does face mean?

121. Who are the books?

122. How are the 'dead' judged?

123. Where were death and hell cast?

124. What is the second death?

125. What will you have when you have experienced God in His fullness?

126. Who shall have their part in the lake of fire?

127. List everything that has been revealed to you in this study.

NOTES:

Benediction

My gracious Heavenly Father, I bring before you the person that has just completed this study. Lord, I ask that you move mightily on the seed that has been planted. That it might shortly be quickened and brought to light.

Lord, that in the days to come, the Word of Life will take hold and begin to produce in this vessel. Let their life never be the same. That when they read your Word, it will be new and fresh to them. It will never again be read the same. Bless their household and let this flame spread like wildfire to all that come in contact with them. Amen.

Special Thanks

I want to give special recognition and thanks to someone who, through many ups and downs in our relationship, has become a dear friend to me. She is the grandmother of my children and the first proof reader of my book, Gloria Overlease. My prayer has been that, while proofing this, she would get a glimpse of what I see.

My daughter's daily prayer has been that her grandmother walk into LIFE and experience the *Change*. God has given us a promise that not one prayer would go unanswered. We stand on that Word.

5932285R0

Made in the USA
Charleston, SC
22 August 2010